CHINESE CUISINE

Shanghai Style

作　　　者	林麗華
翻 譯 顧 問	葛潔輝
出　版　者	純青出版社有限公司
	台北市松江路125號5樓
	郵政劃撥12106299
	電話：(02)5074902．5084331
著作財產權人	財團法人味全文化教育基金會
版 權 所 有	局版台業字第3884號
	中華民國83年12月初版發行
印　　　刷	合同美術印刷廠股份有限公司
定　　　價	新台幣貳佰捌拾元整

Author	Lee Hwa Lin
Translation Consultant	Connie Wolhardt
Publisher	Chin Chin Publishing Co., Ltd.
	5th fl., 125, Sung Chiang Rd,
	Taipei, Taiwan, R.O.C.
	TEL:(02)5074902．5084331
Distributor	Wei-Chuan Publishing
	1455 Monterey Pass Rd, #110
	Monterey Park, CA 91754, U.S.A.
	TEL:(213)2613880．2613878
	FAX:(213)2613299
Printer	Ho Tong Art Painting Factory Co., Ltd.
	Printed in Taiwan, R.O.C.
Copyright Holder	Copyright © 1994
	By Wei-Chuan Cultural-Educational Foundation
	First Printing, December, 1994
	ISBN 0-941676-55-2

序

上海菜俗稱江浙菜或浙寧菜，以長江流域揚州為中心，包括浙江省及江蘇省的杭州、蘇州、寧波、徽州、無錫等地菜餚的綜合體，因此上海菜是具有江南風味的菜餚。

一般上海菜以清爽為主，口味大致相同，有些地方味道較偏於甘甜，每種菜都有加糖的習慣，以紅燒見著，如東坡肉、冰糖元蹄、紅燒豆腐……等。大體上來說，上海菜的菜餚味道濃厚，家庭菜式較出色。

由於筆者是台灣人，對於真正道地的上海菜不是很熟悉，因此在出版這本書的過程裡，由收集資料，試做菜餚到試吃味道，不但由味全家政班的老師鼎力相助，同時也請長輩陳浩泰伯伯、盧秀娟伯母及好友葛潔輝女士、謝家蘭小姐提供寶貴意見，並且經過多次的試做及試吃，使得每道菜味道更完美，書的內容更健全。希望這本書的出版，使各位讀者都能享受到簡單易學又純正的上海菜。

林麗華

Foreword

Shanghai Cuisine is commonly known as Je-Jiang or Jiang-Ning Cuisine. Shanghai Cuisine originated on the cities along the Yangtze River, with Yangchow as its center Je-Jiang Province, and Hangchow, Soochow, Ning-Po, Waichow, and Wu Ti of Jiang-Su Province; represent true characteristics of southern Yangtze River cuisine.

Generally, Shanghai Cuisine is light and most of the dishes are similar in flavor; some may be sweeter than the others, but sugar is added in nearly all dishes as a rule. Shanghai Cuisine is renowned for its braising dishes, such as Poet Su Tun Po's Favorite Pork, Pork Butt Braised in Crystal Sauce, Soy Braised Tofu, etc. Generally speaking, Shanghai dishes are stronger in their seasonings than other regional cuisines. Shanghai Cuisine also makes outstanding dishes for family cooking

Since I, the author, was born in Taiwan, I am not culturally familiar with authentic Shanghai Cuisine. In the process of researching and collecting materials for this book, the culinary teachers at Wei-Chuan Cooking School extended their expertise throughout its development. Moreover, I was fortunate to obtain assistance from senior Shanghai family friends, Mr. and Mrs. H. T. Chen, and also from my good friends, Connie K. Wolhardt, and Marina Hsieh. With their invaluable advice, and participation in numerous preparations and tests, this book has been completed with precision and hopefully perfection. I wish that all our readers will find enjoyment in cooking the easy and tasty genuine Shanghai Cuisine dishes contained herein.

Lee Hwa Lin

目錄 · Content

雞肉類 . Chicken

鴨肉類 . Duck

蛋、豆腐類 . Egg & Bean

蔬菜類 . Vegetables

湯類 . Soups

麵點類 . Noodles

量器介紹 · Conversion Table

1 杯 = 236c.c. = 1 cup (1C.)

1 大匙 = 1湯匙 =15c.c. = 1 Tablespoon (1T.)

1 小匙 = 1茶匙 =5c.c. = 1 Teaspoon (1t.)

重量換算 · Measurement Equivalents

1 兩 = 38公克 = $38g$ = $1/12$lb.= $1^1/_3$oz.

2 兩 = 75公克 = $75g$ = $1/_6$lb = $2^2/_3$oz.

3 兩 = 113公克 = $113g$ = $1/_4$lb.= 4oz.

4 兩 = 150公克 = $150g$ = $1/_3$lb.= $5^1/_4$oz.

6 兩 = 225公克 = $225g$ = $1/_2$lb.= 8oz.

8 兩 = 300公克 = $300g$ = $2/_3$lb.= $10^1/_2$oz.

10兩 = 375公克 = $375g$ = $5/_6$lb.= $13^1/_6$oz.

12兩 = 450公克 = $450g$ = 1 lb.= 16oz.

16兩 = 600公克 = $600g$ = $1^1/_3$lbs.= 21oz. = 1 斤

lb.=pound   g =gram   oz.=ounce

材料的前處理

蔥段的切法 · Green Onion Sections

1 蔥洗淨。
2 去頭、尾部分。
3 切成 3 公分長段。

1 Wash the green onion.
2 Trim off the tops and roots.
3 Cut into 3 cm (1¼") long sections.

1

2

3

烏參的發法 · Dried Sea Cucumber

1 乾烏參洗淨,泡水 1 天,隔天換水煮開,煮開後熄火浸泡,待水涼再換水煮開,熄火浸泡,如此 1 天三次,連續發 2 天至軟。
2 由腹部剪開,取出內臟洗淨加水煮開,再發 1 天即可。

1 Wash the dried sea cucumber, soak in water for one day. Place the sea cucumber into new water and bring the water to a boil. When the water is cooled, change again to new water; bring to another boil. Repeat the process 3 times a day for 2 days, until the sea cucumber turns soft.
2 Snip open lengthwise and clean out the intestines. Cover it with water and bring to a boil. Remove from heat and let it sit for one more day. Then it is ready for cooking.

1

2

百頁的處理 · Bean Curd Sheets (Pai Yeh)

1 水 4 杯,加小蘇打 1 小匙,拌勻使之溶解,即為鹼水。
2 百頁一片片撥開後,入鹼水中泡至變白。
3 取出,入冷水中漂洗至滑感消失即可。

1 Mix 4C. water and 1t. baking soda well until it dissolves.
2 Spread the bean curd sheets one by one and soak in the baking soda solution until color turns white.
3 Remove, rinse under the cold water until no grease remains.

1

2

3

蟹的清洗方法 · Crab

1 將蟹的大螯剪斷，或用筷子插入蟹的內臟，待其氣斷。
2 將蟹殼洗刷乾淨。
3 掀起殼蓋，去掉蓋內之腸泥及蟹鰓，再洗淨即可。

1 Snip off the big claws, and pierce the crab with a chopstick.
2 Brush clean the outer shell.
3 Pull open the top shell, discard the inner dirt and gills. Wash clean.

1

2

3

香菇的處理 · Dried Black Mushrooms

1 香菇用溫水泡軟再洗淨。
2 去蒂頭即可。

1 Soften the mushrooms in warm water, rinse.
2 Discard the stems.

1

2

中式火腿的處理 · Chinese Ham

1 火腿修去旁邊泛黃部份。
2 入冷水中泡15分鐘後，刷去表面之污黴，即為洗淨。
3 火腿放在盤子上，蓋上蓋子，入鍋蒸至皮軟即可。（若是陳年火腿，則先蒸1小時後，倒掉其黃色油汁，再重新蓋好，續蒸至皮軟。）
■ 中式火腿有陳年火腿、中陳火腿及新火腿三種，陳年火腿是指醃製1年以上的火腿，中陳火腿是指醃製6個月至1年的火腿，新火腿是指醃製6個月以下之火腿。新火腿又名家鄉肉或鹹肉。

1 Trim off the yellow parts along the side of the Chinese ham.
2 Soak in cold water for 15 minutes; scrape off the remnants on the surface and wash.
3 Arrange Chinese ham in a shallow plate, cover. Steam until the skin turns soft (if the Chinese ham is aged Chinese ham, steam for 1 hour first; pour out the yellow oil, cover and steam again until skin has softened).
■ There are 3 different types of Chinese ham: aged Chinese ham, medium aged Chinese ham, and new Chinese ham. Aged Chinese ham has been salted for more than one year. Medium aged Chinese ham has been salted between six months to a year. New Chinese ham, also called salted pork, has been salted for less than six months.

1

2

3

特殊材料的製作

凍豆腐的製作 · Frozen Bean Curd

1 豆腐洗淨，入冷凍庫中冰凍至結凍後，取出退冰即為凍豆腐。

1 Wash the bean curd, place in freezer until frozen. Remove and defrost.

1

椒鹽的製作 · Szechwan Pepper Salt

1 鹽1大匙加花椒粉$^1/_2$小匙及味精$^1/_8$小匙，入炒鍋中炒至淡咖啡色即可。

1 Stir-Fry 1T. salt and $^1/_2$t. Szechwan peppercorns powder in a wok until salt turns to light brown.

1

雞油的製作 · Chicken Fat

1 由雞肉取下之肥油洗淨後置碗中，入蒸鍋蒸至溶化即為雞油。

1 Remove the chicken fat from the chicken. Wash, then steam until it becomes liquid.

1

高湯的製作 · Stock

1 以豬、牛、雞的肉或骨入沸水中川燙。
2 再將肉或骨頭取出洗淨。
3 以另一鍋水燒開後，再入洗淨的肉或骨頭，並加少許蔥、薑、酒慢火熬出來的湯，謂之高湯。

1 Parboil pork, beef, chicken or bones.
2 Lift out and wash clean.
3 Bring new clean water to a boil, add the meat or the bones together with some green onion, ginger, and cooking wine. Simmer over low heat until the soup is tasty.

1

2

3

餛飩的包法 · Wontons

1 餛飩皮包上 1 份餡，對折成三角形。
2 再向上對折成半。
3 兩角對疊成型。

1 Fill each wonton wrapper with 1 serving of filling, then fold into triangular shape.
2. Fold the wonton wrappers in half.
3 Pinch together the two corners.

1

2

3

蔬菜切法 · Cutting Vegetables

切片：胡蘿蔔片、香菇片。
切絲：紅辣椒絲、薑絲。
切丁：洋蔥丁、胡蘿蔔丁、筍丁。
切末：蒜末、紅辣椒末。

Cut to slices: carrot slices, black mushroom slices.
Shred: shredded red chili pepper, shredded ginger.
Cut in cubes: onion cubes, carrot cubes, bamboo shoot cubes.
Mince: minced garlic, minced red chili pepper.

1

2

3

4

11

西湖醋魚
West Lake Vinaigrette Fish

草魚 .... 6 0 0 公克		600g(1¹/₃ lbs.) .... grass fish
嫩薑絲 .... 3 0 公克		30g(1oz.) shredded tender ginger
麻油 .... 1 大匙		1T. .... sesame oil

1
- 蔥段 .... 1 5 段
- 薑片 .... 3 片
- 紹興酒 .... 1 大匙

1
- •15 sections green onion
- •3 slices ginger
- •1T. Chinese Shao-Shin wine

2
- 鎮江醋 .... 4 大匙
- 糖 .... 3 ¹/₂ 大匙
- 醬油 .... 3 大匙
- 鹽 .... ¹/₂ 小匙

2
- •4T. brown vinegar
- •3¹/₂ T. sugar
- •3T. soy sauce
- •¹/₂ t. salt

3
- 水 .... 2 小匙
- 太白粉 .... 1 小匙

3
- •2t. water
- •1t. cornstarch

1 草魚洗淨後，從腹部切開，使魚成為背部相連之一大片（圖１），並在兩面魚肉厚處各切三斜刀備用（圖２）。

2 水８杯加**1**料煮開，入草魚（草魚入鍋時，魚背朝上）（圖３），煮開後改小火續煮至魚肉全熟（即魚眼球變白而突出時），熄火立即撈出裝在長盤內，並灑上薑絲，留魚汁１杯備用。

3 **2**料加魚汁煮開，以**3**料芶芡，再加麻油拌勻，淋在魚身上即可。

1 Wash and cut the grass fish open from stomach lengthwise, then flare it open (Fig. 1). Score the fish with 3 diagonal slashes on both sides of the fish (Fig. 2).

2 Bring 8C. water and **1** to a boil; drop in the grass fish (skin side up, Fig. 3) and bring to a boil; reduce to low heat and cook until fish is done (fish eyes turn white and protrude). Turn off heat, remove the fish and place on an oval plate immediately. Spread shredded ginger on the fish. Keep 1C. of fish soup for later use.

3 Bring **2** and fish soup to a boil, thicken with **3** . Mix in sesame oil evenly, pour over the grass fish and serve.

1

2   3

苔托黃魚
Seaweed Flavored Yellow Fish

黃魚（淨肉）	3 3 0	公克
胡椒鹽	2	大匙
苔菜（圖1）	1	大匙

1
蔥段	1 0	段
薑片	1 0	片
水		1/2 杯
紹興酒	1	大匙
鹽	1	小匙
胡椒粉		1/8 小匙

2
低筋麵粉	1	杯
水		1/2 杯
油	1 1/2	大匙
苔菜	1	大匙
泡打粉	1 1/2	小匙
鹽		1/4 小匙
蛋	1	個

330g(11²/₃ oz,net weight)
.... yellow fish fillet
2T. .... pepper salt
1T. .. fine green seaweed
(Fig. 1)

1
- •10 sections green onion
- •10 slices ginger
- •¹/₂C. water
- •1T. Chinese Shao-Shin wine
- •1t. salt
- •¹/₈t. pepper

2
- •1C. low gluten flour
- •¹/₂C. water
- •1¹/₂T. oil
- •1T. fine green seaweed
- •1¹/₂t. baking powder
- •¹/₄t. salt
- •1 egg

1 魚肉切成 1 × 4 公分之條狀，以 **1** 料醃 3 0 分鐘備用。
2 **2** 料調勻成麵糊，將醃好的魚條均勻裹上麵糊（圖2）。鍋熱入油 8 杯燒至九分熱（2 0 0 ℃），入魚條炸至膨發隨即撈出，待所有魚條都炸完後，再將全部魚條回鍋以大火炸至金黃色撈出，最後灑上苔菜拌勻即可。食時可沾胡椒鹽。

1 Cut the fish into 1 cm x 4 cm (¹/₂"x1¹/₂") strips, marinate with **1** for 30 minutes.
2 Mix **2** to a smooth batter. Coat the marinated fish with the batter (Fig. 2). Heat the wok, add 8C. oil and heat to 200℃ (390˚F). Deep-fry the fish until puffy, remove from oil. Return all the fish pieces to the wok and fry over high heat until golden. Remove from oil and drain. Sprinkle on the fine green seaweed and mix thoroughly. May be served with pepper salt.

1

2

海蜇皮拌蘿蔔絲

Cold Appetizer: Jelly Fish with Turnips

白蘿蔔絲 300公克
海蜇皮（圖1）150公克
蔥末、麻油......各1大匙
鹽 ....¹/₂小匙

1
醬油 .... 2 大匙
麻油 .... 1 大匙
糖 .... 2 小匙
白醋 .... 1 小匙

300g(10¹/₂oz.) . shredded
turnip
150g(5¹/₄oz.) ..... jelly fish
(Fig. 1)
1T. each: minced green
onion, sesame oil
¹/₂t. ....salt

1
•2T. soy sauce
•1T. sesame oil
•2t. sugar
•1t. white vinegar

1 海蜇皮切細絲，用冷水泡4小時（每隔1小時換水一次）後，用60℃溫開水10杯直接沖燙（圖2），再瀝乾備用。
2 白蘿蔔絲加鹽醃15分鐘後擠乾水份，上置蔥末。另麻油燒熱，淋在蔥末與蘿蔔絲上，再入海蜇皮、**1** 料拌勻即可。
■ 海蜇皮因質地不同，泡水所需的時間亦有差異，泡水2小時後可試其柔軟度，若柔軟度已夠，可以不必再泡水，若不夠則繼續泡至所需的柔軟度為止（每隔半小時試一次）。

1 Cut the jelly fish into fine threads, soak in cold water for 4 hours (change water every 1 hour). Lower the sieve into 10C. of 60°C (140°F) warm water (Fig. 2), drain.
2 Marinate the turnip with salt for 15 minutes, squeeze out the liquid, then arrange on a plate. Sprinkle with green onion, then pour the heated sesame oil on top. Mix in the jelly fish and **1** thoroughly. Serve.
■ The length of time for soaking the jelly fish may vary due to the differences in the quality of jelly fish. Soak the jelly fish in water for 2 hours then check the tenderness. If the jelly fish is still hard, soak until softened (check again every half an hour).

1

2

爆醃臘魚
Cured Fish Fingers

草魚 ６００公克	600g(1¹/₃ lbs.) .... grass fish

1
- 青蒜絲 .. １２０公克
- 紅辣椒絲 ... １５公克
- 紹興酒 ３大匙
- 鹽 １大匙

1
- •120g(4¹/₄ oz.) shredded garlic leek
- •15g(¹/₂oz.) shredded red chili pepper
- •3T. Chinese Shao-Shin wine
- •1T. salt

1 草魚洗淨，去大刺後切２×５公分條狀，入 **1** 料醃６天，期間經常翻動，使醃拌更均勻。
2 鍋熱入油６杯燒至七分熱（１６０℃），入魚條以中火炸熟，續入剩餘 **1** 料炸酥，再撈出瀝乾油份即可。

1 Wash the grass fish, remove large fish bones and cut into 2 cm x5 cm (1"x2") strips. Marinate with **1** for 6 days. Turn from time to time.
2 Heat the wok, add 6C. oil and heat to 160°C (320°F). Deep-fry the fish strips over medium heat until cooked; add **1**, deep-fry until crispy. Remove from oil and drain. Serve.

龍井蝦仁
Stir-fried Shrimp with Green Tea Leaves

劍蝦 ６００公克	600g(1¹/₃ lbs.) .... shrimp
龍井茶葉 １大匙	1T. ......Lung-Ging green tea leaves
蔥段 １０段	10 sections .... green onion
薑片 １０片	10 slices .... ginger

1
- 蛋白 .... ¹/₂個
- 太白粉 １小匙
- 鹽、味精 ..... 各少許

1
- •¹/₂ egg white
- •1t. cornstarch
- •dash of salt

1 劍蝦去殼去腸泥洗淨，擦乾水份，入 **1** 料醃１０分鐘，龍井茶葉入冷開水中泡開取出瀝乾備用。
2 鍋熱入油¹/₂杯燒至七分熱（１６０℃），入蝦仁炒熟撈出，瀝乾油份。
3 鍋內留油１大匙，入蔥段、薑片炒香後，取出蔥、薑，續入蝦仁及龍井茶葉拌勻即可。

1 Shell and devein the shrimp with toothpicks; wash and pat dry. Marinate with **1** for 10 minutes. Soak tea leaves in cold water until leaves have opened. Drain and keep the tea leaves to use later.
2 Heat the wok, add ¹/₂C. oil and heat to 160°C (320°F). Stir-fry the shrimp until cooked; remove from oil and drain.
3 Keep 1T. oil in the wok, stir-fry the green onions and ginger until fragrant, discard both. In the remaining oil, stir-fry the shrimp and tea leaves, mix well. Serve.

Stir-fried Shrimp with Ginkgo Nuts

劍蝦 ６００公克
白果罐頭（圖１）... １罐
蔥段 １０段
薑片 １０片
麻油 １小匙

1 ─┌ 蛋白 .... ½個
　　│ 太白粉 １小匙
　　│ 鹽 .... ½小匙
　　└ 味精 .... ⅛小匙

600g(1⅓lbs.) ..... shrimp
1 can .... ginkgo nuts
(Fig. 1)
10 sections .... green onion
10 slices .... ginger
1t. .... sesame oil

1 ─┌ •½ egg white
　　│ •1t. cornstarch
　　└ •½t. salt

1 劍蝦去殼去腸泥（圖２）洗淨，擦乾水份（圖３），入**1**料醃１０分鐘，白果以熱開水燙過瀝乾備用。
2 鍋熱入油½杯燒至七分熱（１６０℃），入劍蝦仁炒熟撈出，瀝乾油份。
3 鍋內留油２大匙，入蔥段、薑片炒香後，取出蔥、薑，續入白果、蝦仁拌炒均勻，並淋上麻油即可。

1 Shell and devein the shrimp (Fig. 2); wash and pat dry (Fig. 3). Marinate with **1** for 10 minutes. Blanch the ginkgo nuts in boiling water, remove and drain.
2 Heat the wok, add ½C. oil and heat to 160°C (320°F). Stir-fry the shrimp until cooked; remove from oil and drain.
3 Keep 2T. oil in the wok; stir-fry the green onions and ginger until fragrant, discard both. In the remaining oil, stir-fry the ginkgo nuts and shrimp, mix well. Sprinkle on the sesame oil and serve.

1

2

3

醬爆蟹
Stir-fried Crab in Bean Paste Sauce

青蟹 ９００公克
毛豆仁 ２５公克
麵粉 .... ¼ 杯
蔥末、薑末 各３大匙
甜麵醬、番茄醬、麻油 ...
.... 各１大匙

1
蔥段 ５段
薑片 ５片
紹興酒 １大匙
鹽 .... ¼ 小匙

2
水 .... ½ 杯
紹興酒 １大匙
醬油、糖 ... 各２小匙

900g(2lbs.) .... crabs
25g(1oz.) .... fresh soy beans
¼C. .... flour
3T. each: minced green onion, minced ginger
1T. each: sweet soy bean paste, ketchup, sesame oil

1
- 5 sections green onion
- 5 slices ginger
- 1T. Chinese Shao-Shin wine
- ¼t. salt

2
- ½C. water
- 1T. Chinese Shao-Shin wine
- 2t. each: soy sauce, sugar

1 青蟹洗淨，切下蟹螯以刀背拍碎，蟹身切成４塊，入 **1** 料醃２０分鐘備用。
2 鍋熱入油８杯燒至八分熱（１８０℃），將醃好的蟹塊沾上麵粉投入油鍋中炸約１分鐘至熟，隨即撈出瀝乾油份。
3 另鍋熱入油２大匙燒熱，入蔥末、薑末炒香，續入甜麵醬、番茄醬略炒，再加 **2** 料煮開，入蟹塊及毛豆仁炒勻，起鍋前再加麻油拌勻即可。

1 Wash the crabs, snip off the claws and crack the claws with the back of a knife. Cut the crab bodies into 4 pieces, marinate with **1** for 20 minutes.
2 Heat the wok, add 8C. oil and heat to 180°C (360°F). Coat the marinated crabs with flour, deep-fry until cooked (about 1 minute). Remove from oil immediately and drain.
3 Heat the wok, add 2T. oil and heat. Stir-fry the green onions and ginger until fragrant. Stir in the sweet soy bean paste and ketchup, fry slightly. Add **2** and bring to a boil, add the crabs and fresh soy beans, stir-fry thoroughly. Mix in the sesame oil before serving.

蟹肉炒蛋
Crab Meat Egg Foo Yung

青蟹 .... 6 0 0 公克
蛋 .... 4 個
蔥末、薑末、紹興酒 ......
.... 各 1 大匙

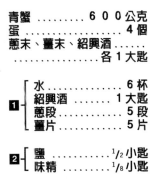

1
水 .... 6 杯
紹興酒 .... 1 大匙
蔥段 .... 5 段
薑片 .... 5 片

2
鹽 .... ¹/₂ 小匙
味精 .... ¹/₈ 小匙

600g(1¹/₃lbs.) ....crabs
4 ....eggs
1T. each: minced green
onion, minced ginger,
Chinese Shao-Shin wine

1
•6C. water
•1T. Chinese Shao-
Shin wine
•5 sections green
onion
•5 slices ginger

2 •¹/₂t. salt

1 青蟹洗淨，切下蟹螯以刀背拍碎，蟹身切成 4 塊（圖 1）。**1**料煮開，入蟹塊煮熟撈出，待涼取出蟹肉（圖 2）備用。
2 鍋熱入油 1 大匙燒熱，入蔥末、薑末炒香，續入蟹肉及紹興酒拌炒均勻，待涼備用。
3 蛋打散，入蟹肉及 **2**料攪拌均勻。鍋熱入油¹/₂ 杯燒熱，入蟹肉蛋液以大火拌炒至蛋液凝固即可。

1 Wash the crabs, snip off the claws and crack the claws with the back of a knife. Cut the crabs into 4 pieces (Fig. 1). Bring **1** to a boil, add the crabs and cook until done. Cool and remove the crab meat (Fig. 2)
2 Heat the wok, add 1T. oil and heat. Stir-fry the green onions and ginger until fragrant. Add the crab meat and Chinese Shao-Shin wine, mix well.
3 Beat the eggs, mix in the crab meat and **2** thoroughly. Heat the wok, add ¹/₂C. oil and heat. Add the crab meat and eggs mixture, stir-fry over high heat until the eggs turn solid.

1　　2

煙燻鯧魚
Smoked Pomfret

鯧魚（淨重）　　５００公克
蔥 . . . . 2 枝
蔥末、麻油 . . . . . . 各2 大匙

1　┌ 蔥段、芹菜段各１０段
　　│ 薑片 . . . . 10 片
　　│ 紹興酒 . . . . 2 大匙
　　│ 鹽 . . . . 1 小匙
　　└ 味精、胡椒粉各$^1/_2$ 小匙

2　┌ 糖、麵粉 各１杯
　　│ 茶葉 . . . . $^1/_2$ 杯
　　│ 米 . . . . $^1/_4$ 杯
　　│ 蔥末、薑末 各2 大匙
　　└ 八角 . . . . 10 顆

500g(1lb.,net weight) ....
pomfret
2 stalks ...... green onion
2T. each: minced green
onion, sesame oil

1　┌ •10 sections each:
　　│ green onion, celery
　　│ •10 slices ginger
　　│ •2T. Chinese Shao-
　　│ Shin wine
　　│ •1t. salt
　　└ •$^1/_2$t. pepper

2　┌ •1C. each: sugar,
　　│ flour
　　│ •$^1/_2$C. tea leaves
　　│ •$^1/_4$C. rice
　　│ •2T. each: minced
　　│ green onion,
　　│ minced ginger
　　└ •10 pieces star anise

1 鯧魚洗淨，切鑽石花（圖１），入 **1** 料醃一夜備用（醃時需翻面使味道均勻）。
2 蔥切對半，墊在乾鍋底，上置醃好的鯧魚，另鍋熱入油 8 杯燒至九分熱（２００℃），沖入鯧魚中（圖２），蓋鍋蓋，將魚泡熟備用。
3 另鍋底入一張鋁箔紙，內置 **2** 料，上置網架，網架上放鯧魚，蓋鍋蓋大火加熱至出現淡黃色煙霧後，改中火燻至上色（約３分鐘），盛入盤內，魚身灑上蔥末，再淋上燒熱的麻油即可。
■ 供食時附上一碟沙拉醬及半個檸檬。

1 Wash the pomfret, cut to diamond shape (Fig. 1). Marinate in **1** overnight (turn frequently).
2 Halve the green onions and place at bottom of a wok. Place the marinated pomfret on top of green onions. Heat another wok, add 8C. oil and heat to 200°C (390°F). Pour hot oil on the pomfret (Fig. 2) then cover the wok and soak the fish until cooked.
3 Line the bottom of a clean wok with aluminum foil; spread **2** on the foil. Place a rack on top. Lay the pomfret on the rack. Cover with a lid. Cook over high heat until yellow smoke rises from the wok. Reduce heat to medium and smoke the fish until color changes to light brown (about 3 minutes). Remove and arrange the fish on a plate. Sprinkle on minced green onion, pour heated sesame oil over the fish.
4 Serve with salad dressing and half of a lemon.

1

2

Braised Sea Cucumber with Shrimp Roe

烏參 ６００公克
蔥末、薑末、蝦子、紹興酒
.... 各１大匙

1
水 ６杯
紹興酒 １大匙
蔥段 ５段
薑片 ５片

2
水 １杯
醬油 ３大匙
糖 １小匙
鹽 .... ¹/₄小匙
胡椒粉 .... ¹/₈小匙

600g(1¹/₃lbs.) .... sea cucumber
1T. each: minced green onion, minced ginger, shrimp roe, Chinese Shao-Shin wine

1
- 6C. water
- 1T. Chinese Shao-Shin wine
- 5 sections green onion
- 5 slices ginger

2
- 1C. water
- 3T. soy sauce
- 1t. sugar
- ¹/₄t. salt
- ¹/₈t. pepper

1 烏參腹內清洗乾淨，**1**料煮開，入烏參煮５分鐘後撈出備用。
2 鍋熱入油１大匙燒熱，入蔥末、薑末爆香，續入蝦子及紹興酒炒香，再入**2**料及烏參煮開，改小火續煮１０分鐘至湯汁濃稠且烏參熟爛即可。
■ 蝦子有兩種：１．乾蝦子呈黑色，顆粒小（圖１），必須加酒蒸過，使其膨發並去腥味。
　　　　　　　２．新鮮蝦子呈暗紅色，顆粒較大（圖２），可不蒸過直接使用。

1 Wash the inner part of the sea cucumber. Bring **1** to a boil, add the sea cucumber and cook for 5 minutes, remove and drain.
2 Heat the wok, add 1T. oil and heat. Fry the green onions and ginger until fragrant. Add the shrimp roe and Chinese Snao-Shin wine, stir-fry until fragrant. Mix in **2** and the sea cucumber, bring to a boil. Reduce to low heat and cook for 10 minutes until sauce thickens and the sea cucumber are very tender.
■ Two types of shrimp roe: 1 The dried shrimp roe is black and smaller (Fig. 1), it needs to be steamed with cooking wine until puffy to reduce the offensive fish smell.
2 The fresh shrimp roe is dark red and bigger (Fig. 2); it doesn't need to be steamed and may be used right away.

1

2

紅燒肚膛
Fish Fillet in Soy Sauce

草魚中段（淨重）........
.... 3 0 0 公克
青蒜絲 .... 5 公克
蔥段 .... 5 段
薑片 .... 5 片
紹興酒 .... 1 大匙
麻油 .... 1 小匙

1［蔥段 .... 5 段
　　薑片 .... 5 片
　　醬油、紹興酒各 1 大匙

2［水 .... 1 杯
　　醬油、糖 ... 各 1 大匙
　　味精 .... 少許

300g(10½oz.,net weight)
grass fish fillet
5g(¼oz.) .... shredded
garlic leek
5 sections ..green onion
5 slices .... ginger
1T. ..Chinese Shao-Shin
wine
1t. .... sesame oil

1［•5 sections green
　　onion
　　•5 slices ginger
　　•1T. each: soy sauce,
　　Chinese Shao-Shin
　　wine

2［•1C. water
　　•1T. each: soy sauce,
　　sugar

1 草魚洗淨，每隔 5 公分劃一刀（圖 1），以**1**料醃 1 小時備用。
2 鍋熱入油 4 大匙燒熱，入蔥段、薑片爆香，續入草魚煎至兩面金黃色，再沿鍋邊入紹興酒（圖 2），最後入醃魚餘汁及**2**料煮開，改小火煮至湯汁濃稠後，取出蔥段、薑片，拌入麻油盛盤，並灑上青蒜絲即可。

1 Wash the fish, score diagonal cuts every 5 cm (2") (Fig. 1). Marinate in **1** for 1 hour.
2 Heat the wok, add 4T. oil and heat. Stir-fry the green onions and ginger until fragrant. Add the grass fish and fry until both sides turn golden brown. Pour in the Chinese Shao-Shin wine along the side of the wok (Fig. 2). Mix in the marinated fish sauce and **2**, bring to a boil. Reduce to low heat and simmer until sauce has thickened. Discard the green onions and ginger. Mix in the sesame oil. Arrange the fish on a plate. Sprinkle on garlic leek and serve.

1

2

劍蝦 ３００公克
鱔魚（淨肉） １５０公克
麵粉 ....¹/₄ 杯
蔥末、薑末 各１大匙
麻油 １小匙

1
蛋白 .... ¹/₄ 個
太白粉 １小匙
鹽 .... 少許

2
水 .... ¹/₄ 杯
紹興酒 １大匙
醬油 ２小匙
糖 １¹/₂小匙
味精 .... 少許

3
水 .... ¹/₂ 小匙
太白粉 ...... ¹/₄ 小匙

300g(10¹/₂oz.) ..... shrimp
150g(5¹/₄oz., net weight)
baby eels
¹/₄C. ....flour
**1T. each: minced green
onion, minced ginger**
1t. ....sesame oil

1
- •¹/₄ egg white
- •1t. cornstarch
- •dash of salt

2
- •¹/₄C. water
- •1T. Chinese Shao-
  Shin wine
- •2t. soy sauce
- •1¹/₂t. sugar

3
- •¹/₂t. water
- •¹/₄t. cornstarch

1 劍蝦去殼去腸泥洗淨，擦乾水份，入 **1** 料醃１０分鐘備用。
2 鱔魚切成５公分段（圖１），沾麵粉備用（圖２）。
3 鍋熱入油¹/₂杯燒至七分熱（１６０C），入劍蝦仁炒熟，撈出瀝乾油份，續入油６杯燒至八分熱（１８０℃），入鱔魚炸至酥脆撈出瀝乾油份，與蝦仁混合均勻備用。
4 鍋熱入油１大匙燒熱，入蔥末、薑末爆香，續入 **2** 料煮開，以 **3** 料芶芡，再入麻油、鱔魚、蝦仁拌勻即可。

1 Shell and devein the shrimp, pat dry. Marinate in **1** for 10 minutes.
2 Cut the baby eels into 5 cm (2") sections (Fig. 1), coat with flour (Fig. 2).
3 Heat the wok, add ¹/₂C. oil and heat to 160°C (320°F). Fry the shrimp until done, remove from oil and drain. Add 6C. oil and heat to 180°C (360°F). Deep-fry the baby eels until crispy, remove from oil and drain. Mix well with the shrimp.
4 Heat the wok, add 1T. oil and heat. Stir-fry the green onions and ginger until fragrant. Stir in **2** and bring to a boil; thicken with **3**. Add the sesame oil, baby eels, and shrimp. Mix well and serve.

1

2

砂鍋魚頭
Stewed Fish Head Casserole

魚頭（1個） 600公克
粉皮（圖1） 130公克
青蒜絲（圖2） 60公克
中式火腿 ⋯⋯⋯ 30公克
辣豆瓣醬 ⋯⋯⋯⋯ 1大匙
胡椒粉 ⋯⋯⋯⋯⋯ 1/8小匙
凍豆腐 ⋯⋯⋯⋯⋯ 1塊
蔥段 ⋯⋯⋯⋯⋯⋯ 8段
薑片 ⋯⋯⋯⋯⋯⋯ 5片

1 醬油、酒 ⋯⋯各1大匙

2
水 ⋯⋯⋯⋯⋯ 6杯
醬油 ⋯⋯⋯⋯ 5大匙
酒、糖 ⋯⋯各1大匙

600g(1¹/₃lbs.,1) fish head
130g(4¹/₂oz.) ⋯⋯⋯mung
bean sheets (Fig. 1)
60g(2oz.) shredded garlic leek (Fig. 2)
30g(1oz.) ..Chinese ham
1T. ..hot soy bean paste
¹/₈t. ⋯⋯⋯⋯⋯⋯pepper
1 square ⋯⋯frozen bean curd
8 sections ..green onion
5 slices ⋯⋯⋯⋯ginger

1 •1T. each: soy sauce, cooking wine

2
•6C. water
•5T. soy sauce
•1T. each: cooking wine, sugar

1 魚頭洗淨，以**1**料醃20分鐘後，入8分熱（180℃）油鍋炸至兩面呈金黃色取出，凍豆腐切成12塊，粉皮切片，中式火腿洗淨蒸熟切片，備用。

2 砂鍋燒熱入油1大匙燒熱，入辣豆瓣醬、薑片及蔥段炒香，續入魚頭、中式火腿、**2**料及凍豆腐煮開，改小火煮40分鐘，再入粉皮續煮5分鐘，熄火灑上胡椒粉及青蒜絲即可。

1 Wash the fish head, marinate in **1** for 20 minutes, remove. Deep-fry the fish head in the wok in 180°C (360°F) oil until both sides turn golden brown; remove from the wok. Cut the bean curd into 12 pieces; slice the mung bean sheets to serving size. Wash and steam the ham; cut into serving slices.

2 Heat a ceramic pot, add 1T. oil and heat. Stir-fry the hot soy bean paste, ginger, and green onions until fragrant. Add the fish head, ham, **2**, and bean curd; bring to a boil. Reduce to low heat and simmer for 40 minutes. Add the mung bean sheets and simmer for 5 more minutes. Turn off heat and sprinkle with pepper and garlic leek. Serve hot.

1

2

蔥烤鯽魚
Gold Carp Topped with Green Onions

鯽魚(淨重)...５００公克
蔥..........３００公克

1
冰糖、醬油...各¹/₄杯
白醋.........５大匙
味精.........¹/₂小匙

500g(1lb.) .....gold carps
300g(10¹/₂oz.) ....green
onions

1
•¹/₄C. each: crystal
sugar, soy sauce
•5T. white vinegar

1 鯽魚、蔥均洗淨，蔥切１０公分長段備用。
2 鍋熱入油６杯燒至八分熱（１８０℃），入蔥段炸至表面稍黃，撈起備用。餘油再加熱，續入鯽魚以大火炸酥，撈出瀝乾油份，以 **1** 料醃泡３小時（浸泡時每隔半小時翻面一次，使魚均勻浸泡）。
3 取¹/₃炸過的蔥段墊在鍋底（圖１），上置鯽魚（圖２），再放上剩餘的蔥，並淋下醃魚所剩之汁液，加水１杯煮開後，蓋上鍋蓋改小火續燒煮１小時至湯汁收乾，待涼即可供食。

1 Wash the green onions and gold carps. Cut the green onions into 10 cm (4") long sections.
2 Heat the wok, add 6C. oil and heat to 180°C (360°F). Deep-fry the green onions until lightly browned; remove from oil. Heat the remaining oil, deep-fry the gold carps over high heat until crispy, remove from oil and drain. Marinate the gold carp with **1** for 3 hours (turn every half hour to destribute the flavor).
3 Place ¹/₃ of the fried green onions at the bottom of the wok (Fig. 1). Put the gold carps on top of the green onions (Fig. 2), then arrange the remaining green onions on top of the gold carps; then top with the remaining marinating sauce. Add 1C. water, bring to a boil, cover. Reduce to low heat and simmer for 1 hour, until sauce evaporates. Cool and serve.

1

2

方塊肉
Pork Squares in Brown Sauce

五花肉（7×13公分長方塊）
.... 500公克
醬油 2大匙

1
- 水.... .... 6 杯
- 冰糖、紹興酒 .... 各½ 杯
- 醬油 .... ⅓ 杯
- 蔥段 .... 12 段
- 薑片 .... 6 片

500g(1lb.) ....pork belly
(7x13cm or 2¾"x5" square)
2T. ....soy sauce

1
- •6C. water
- •½C. each: crystal sugar,
  Chinese Shao-Shin wine
- •⅓C. soy sauce
- •12 sections green onion
- •6 slices ginger

1 五花肉洗淨置鍋（肉皮朝下，圖1），入醬油將肉皮煎至焦黃色（圖2），取出入冷水泡涼，再用湯匙把焦黑處刮去（圖3）備用。
2 肉加 **1** 料大火煮開，改中火煮 2 小時，再改小火慢煮，並不時地將湯汁澆淋在肉上，直至湯汁剩 1 杯即可。

1 Wash the pork, place in a wok (skin side down, Fig. 1). Fry the pork in soy sauce until the skin turns golden brown (Fig. 2); remove, soak in cold water until cool. Use a spoon to scrape off the burned sections (Fig. 3).
2 Add **1** to the pork, bring to a boil over high heat. Reduce to medium heat and cook for 2 hours. Reduce to low heat and simmer, spooning the sauce over the pork constantly until sauce is reduced to 1C. Serve.

1

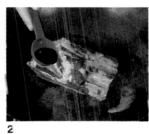

2

3

無錫排骨
Wu She Pork Ribs

里肌肋排（去除厚肉部份如圖 1）．．．．．．．４５０公克

1 醬油 ．．．．．．．．．１ 大匙
　　小蘇打 ．．．．．．．¹/₂ 小匙

2 高湯 ．．．．．．．．．．．．１ 杯
　　醬油 ．．．．．．．．．．．２ 大匙
　　冰糖 ．．．．．．．．．．．１ 大匙
　　薑片 ．．．．．．．．．．．．．７ 片

3 高湯 ．．．．．．．．．．．．．¹/₂ 杯
　　酒 ．．．．．．．．．．．．．．¹/₄ 杯

450g(1lb.) .... pork ribs
(Fig. 1)

1
- •1T. soy sauce
- •¹/₂t. baking soda

2
- •1C. stock
- •2T. soy sauce
- •1T. crystal sugar
- •7 slices ginger

3
- •¹/₂C. stock
- •¹/₄C. cooking wine

1 肋排洗淨擦乾水份，入 **1** 料醃 5 分鐘備用。
2 鍋熱入油 5 杯燒至八分熱（１８０℃），入肋排炸至金黃色（圖 2 ，約 5 分鐘）撈起瀝油備用。
3 **2** 料煮沸，入肋排煮沸再改小火燒煮至湯汁剩約¹/₂杯，再加 **3** 料續煮至肉軟，湯汁剩約 3 大匙即可。

1 Wash the ribs, pat dry, marinate in **1** for 5 minutes.
2 Heat the wok, add 5C. oil and heat to 180°C (360°F). Deep-fry the ribs until golden brown, about 5 minutes (Fig. 2). Remove from oil and drain.
3 Bring **2** to a boil add the ribs and bring to another boil. Reduce to low heat and simmer until only ¹/₂C. of the sauce remains. Add **3** and cook until the ribs become tender and sauce has been reduced to 3T. Serve.

1

2

五花肉 ６００公克
棉繩 .... 3 條

1
- 蔥段 ２０段
- 薑片(厚) ...... 5 片
- 八角 .... 2 顆
- 紹興酒 .... 1 杯
- 醬油 .... 5 大匙
- 桂皮(圖1)... ½ 小匙

2
- 水 .... 2 杯
- 冰糖 .... ½ 杯

600g(1⅓lbs.) pork belly
3 pieces .... cotton string

1
- •20 sections green onion
- •5 slices (thick) ginger
- •2 pieces star anise
- •1C. Chinese Shao-Shin wine
- •5T. soy sauce
- •½t. cinnamon (Fig. 1)

2
- •2C. water
- •½C. crystal sugar

1 五花肉置於冰箱冷凍定型後，切成３．５公分立方塊，取棉繩綑成十字型（圖２）加以固定備用。
2 **1**料煮開，入五花肉大火煮屌，改小火煮５０分鐘熄火，倒入大碗內，加**2**料再入鍋蒸 2½ 小時，取出撈除表面浮油即可。

1 Place the pork belly in freezer until frozen, cut into 3.5 cm (1½") squares. Tie the pork squares with the strings (Fig. 2).
2 Bring **1** to a boil, add pork, bring to a boil over high heat. Reduce to low heat and simmer for 50 minutes. Remove from heat and pour into a big soup bowl. Add **2**, steam for 2½ hours. Skim the fat off the surface, serve.

1

2

腐乳肉
Braised Pork in Preserved Bean Curd Sauce

五花肉 600公克

1
水 .... 2 杯
紅豆腐乳汁 3 1/2 大匙
紹興酒、冰糖各 2 大匙
紅豆腐乳（圖 1 ）2 塊
食用紅色素 ..... 少許
蔥段 .... 12 段
薑片 .... 6 片

600g(1 1/3 lbs.) . pork belly

1
- 2C. water
- 3 1/2 T. juice from preserved red bean curd
- 2T. each: Chinese Shao-Shin wine, crystal sugar
- 2 pieces preserved red bean curd (Fig. 1)
- few drops of red coloring
- 12 sections green onion
- 6 slices ginger

1 五花肉洗淨，入水中煮 25 分鐘（水需蓋過肉），撈起泡冷水至涼瀝乾，在肉皮上用刀劃成 2 公分正方的小格備用（圖 2 ）。
2 取 1 個大碗將 **1** 料拌勻，入五花肉，蓋上保鮮膜（圖 3 ），入鍋蒸 2 小時後取出，倒入另一鍋中，挑去蔥、薑，用小火燜煮至湯汁剩 1/2 杯（約 1 小時）即可。

1 Wash the pork belly, cook in boiling water for 25 minutes (water should cover the pork); remove. Cool in cold water, drain; score 2 cm (1") squares on the skin of pork belly (Fig. 2).
2 Mix **1** in a large bowl thoroughly, add the pork belly; cover with cellophane paper and steam for 2 hours, remove. Transfer the pork to another pot, discard the green onions and ginger, then simmer over low heat until sauce is reduced to 1/2C. (about 1 hour). Serve.

1

2

3

Pork with Preserved Mustard Greens

五花肉 ６０ ０公克
梅干菜 ８ ０公克
冰糖 .... ３ ¹/₂ 大匙

1 醬油、酒 各２大匙

600g(1¹/₃lbs.) . pork belly
80g(2³/₄oz.) ....preserved
mustard greens
3¹/₂T. ....crystal sugar

1 ⎰ •2T. each: soy sauce,
　　⎱ cooking wine

1

2

3

1 五花肉洗淨，以 **1** 料醃 5 分鐘後，入油鍋炸至金黃色（炸時皮朝下，油鍋的油只需泡到肥肉處，瘦肉不需炸）（圖 1），撈起浸泡於冰水中（圖 2，此種方式稱走油）。
2 取出肉塊，切成 1．5×9 公分片狀，表面再刷上剩餘之 **1** 料；梅干菜洗淨切碎，均備用。
3 取一扣碗，將五花肉片鋪在碗內（圖 3）再入梅干菜，最後灑上冰糖，以保鮮膜封口入鍋蒸 3 小時，取出倒扣於盤上即可。
■ 梅干菜的品質不同，若太鹹則洗淨後再泡水片刻，以降低鹹味。

1 Wash the pork, marinate in **1** for 5 minutes. Deep-fry the pork until color changes to golden brown. (Deep-fry with skin side down. Oil should only cover the skin and fat. Do not fry the lean pork.) (Fig. 1). Remove from oil, soak in ice water (Fig. 2).
2 Remove the pork from ice water, cut into 1.5 cm x 9 cm (¹/₂"x3¹/₂") pieces. Brush the surface with the marinade **1**. Wash and mince the preserved mustard greens.
3 Arrange the pork neatly in a bowl (Fig. 3), spread the preserved mustard greens on top. Sprinkle with crystal sugar, cover the bowl with cellophane paper, and steam for 3 hours. Remove the paper and invert the bowl on a serving plate.
■ The quality of preserved mustard greens varies. If the preserved mustard greens are too salty, wash and soak in water to reduce the saltiness.

紅燒獅子頭
Braised Lions' Heads

絞肉、大白菜各６００公克

1
- 蛋 . . . . 1 個
- 醬油 . . . . 3 大匙
- 油、酒、麻油各 1 大匙
- 糖 . . . . 1 小匙
- 薑泥、胡椒粉各 1/4 小匙

2
- 高湯 . . . . 2 杯
- 醬油 . . . . 1 1/2 大匙
- 冰糖 . . . . 1 小匙

3
- 水 . . . . 3 大匙
- 太白粉 . . . . 2 大匙

600g(1¹/₃lbs.) each: ....
ground pork, Chinese
cabbage

1
- •1 egg
- •3T. soy sauce
- •1T. each: cooking
  wine, sesame oil,
  oil
- •1t. sugar
- •¹/₄t. each: ginger
  paste, pepper

2
- •2C. stock
- •1¹/₂T. soy sauce
- •1t. crystal sugar

3
- •3T. water
- •2T. cornstarch

1 絞肉加 **1** 料攪拌並摔打均勻後，分成 4 等份，再搓成圓球狀，每份肉球表面沾裹已調勻之 **3** 料備用。

2 鍋熱入油 4 杯燒至二分熱（６０℃），入肉球炸至表面呈金黃色即可撈起瀝油備用。

3 白菜一片片剝下洗淨後，留 4 大片，其餘置於砂鍋底層（圖 1 ），上面放上肉球（圖 2 ），再覆上 4 片白菜，最後加 **2** 料煮開後，改小火燉煮 1 小時即可。

1 Mix the ground pork with **1**, throw the meat against a counter or cutting board several times (this improves the texture), then divide into 4 equal portions. Roll into four meat balls, coat the surface with well-mixed **3**.

2 Heat the wok, add 4C. oil and heat to 60°C (140°F). Deep-fry the meat balls until golden brown; remove from oil and drain.

3 Peel off the cabbage leaf by leaf, wash clean. Keep four large cabbage leaves, place the rest of the cabbage at the bottom of a ceramic pot (Fig. 1). Arrange the meat balls on top of the cabbage (Fig. 2), cover with the four cabbage leaves. Add **2** and bring to a boil, reduce to low heat and simmer for 1 hour. Serve.

1

2

Spicy Eight Treasures Pork in Bean Paste Sauce

豆干 100公克
梅花肉、雞胸肉、熟筍、青
椒 各70公克
花生 50公克
蝦米 20公克
香菇 9公克
高湯 .... 1/4 杯
雞肫 .... 2 個

1 醬油、太白粉 各1小匙

2 辣豆瓣醬 2大匙
豆瓣醬、甜麵醬 .....
.... 各1大匙

3 高湯 .... 1/2 杯
糖 .... 2 小匙

100g(3^1/$_2$oz.) .... dried
bean curd
70g(2^1/$_2$oz.) each: pork
shoulder,chicken breast,
boiled bamboo shoots,
green peppers
50g(1^3/$_4$oz.) .... peanuts
20g(^{2}/$_3$oz.) ..... dried baby
shrimp
9g(^{1}/$_3$oz.) ...... dried black
mushrooms
1/4C. .... stock
2 pieces .... chicken
gizzard

1 •1t. each: soy sauce,
cornstarch

2 •2T. hot soy bean
paste
•1T. each: soy bean
paste, sweet soy
bean paste

3 •1/2C. stock
•2t. sugar

1 梅花肉洗淨切1立方公分小丁，入**1**料醃10分鐘；香菇泡軟洗淨去蒂，青椒去籽洗淨，與雞胸肉、豆干、雞肫、筍均切1立方公分小丁；花生、蝦米洗淨備用。
2 鍋熱入油1杯燒至四分熱（100℃），入雞丁、肉丁、雞肫及青椒炒熟取出備用。
3 鍋熱入油3大匙燒熱，入**2**料爆香，續入豆干拌炒數下，再入其餘材料及**3**料，小火燜煮至湯汁快乾，再入高湯續燒至湯汁剩1大匙即可。

1 Wash and cut the pork into 1 cm (^{1}/$_2$") cubes, marinate with **1** for 10 minutes. Soak the mushrooms until soft, discard the stems. Remove the seeds in green peppers, wash. Cut the mushrooms, green peppers, bean curd, chicken, chicken gizzards, and bamboo shoots into 1 cm (1/2") cubes: rinse the peanuts and dried baby shrimp.
2 Heat the wok, add 1C. oil and heat to 100°C (212°F). Stir-fry the chicken, pork, chicken gizzards, and green peppers until cooked; remove.
3 Heat the wok, add 3T. oil and heat. Fry **2** until fragrant, stir in the dried bean curd and fry slightly. Mix in the rest of the ingredients and **3**, simmer over low heat until almost dry. Add the stock and cook until sauce is reduced to 1T. Serve.

冰糖元蹄
Braised Pork Shoulder in Crystal Sugar Sauce

蹄膀（1個）1 2 0 0 公克
醬油 . . . . 2 大匙

1
高湯 . . . . 2 杯
醬油 . . . . ¼ 杯
蔥段 . . . . 1 2 段
薑片（厚）. . . . . 3 片

2
紹興酒 . . . . ½ 杯
冰糖 . . . . 3 大匙
醬油 . . . . 2 大匙

1 (1200g or 2½lbs.) ....
pork shoulder
2T. .... soy sauce

1
•2C. stock
•¼C. soy sauce
•12 sections green onion
•3 slices (thick) ginger

2
•½C. Chinese Shao-Shin wine
•3T. crystal sugar
•2T. soy sauce

1 蹄膀洗淨擦乾水份，入醬油塗抹於蹄膀表面備用。
2 鍋熱入油 6 杯燒至八分熱（1 8 0 ℃），入蹄膀炸至表面呈金黃色（圖 1），取出瀝油備用。
3 **1** 料與蹄膀入鍋蒸 2 小時，取出置於鍋中，再入 **2** 料煮開後，改小火煮至湯汁剩 5 大匙即可。

1 Wash the pork shoulder, pat dry; brush with soy sauce.
2 Heat the wok, add 6C. oil and heat to 180°C (360°F). Deep-fry the pork shoulder until golden brown (illus. 1); remove from oil and drain.
3 Steam the pork shoulder with **1** for 2 hours, transfer to a pot. Add **2** and bring to a boil; simmer over low heat until 5T. of the sauce remains. Serve.

1

Braised Pork with Dried Fish

五花肉 ４５０公克
貴魚鯗（圖１）１００公克
高湯 ３杯

1〔蔥段 .... 4 段
　〔薑片（厚）..... 3 片

2〔紹興酒、醬油各２大匙
　〔冰糖 .... 1 大匙

450g(1lb.) ......pork belly
100g(3¹/₂oz.) ...dried fish
(siang yu, Fig. 1)
3C. ....stock

1〔•4 sections green
　 onion
　•3 slices (thick)
　 ginger

2〔•2T. each: Chinese
　 Shao-Shin wine,
　 soy sauce
　•1T. crystal sugar

1 貴魚鯗泡水 5 分鐘後，去反切 2.5×4 公分長方塊（圖 2），五花肉洗淨切 1 公分厚片狀備用。
2 鍋熱入油 3 大匙燒熱，入 **1** 料爆香，續入五花肉炒至金黃色，再入 **2** 料及高湯 2 杯，大火煮開改
　小火煮 3 0 分鐘，最後加入高湯 1 杯及貴魚鯗小火煮 1 小時，取出蔥、薑即可供食。

1　Soak the dried fish in water for 5 minutes, remove the skin, cut into 2.5 cm x 4 cm (1"x1¹/₂")
　pieces (Fig. 2). Wash the pork and cut into 1 cm (¹/₂") thick slices.
2　Heat the wok, add 3T. oil and heat. Fry **1** until fragrant; stir in the pork and fry until golden
　brown. Mix in **2** and 2C. stock, bring to a boil over high heat; reduce to low heat and simmer
　for 30 minutes. Add 1C. stock and dried fish; simmer for another hour. Discard the green
　onions and ginger. Serve.

1

2

蔥烤排骨
Braised Pork with Shallots and Onions

洋蔥 .... 7 5 0 公克	750g(1²/₃lbs.) .... onions	
肋排（五花肉上之部位）... 6 0 0 公克	600g(1¹/₃lbs.) spare ribs (the section above pork belly)	
紅蔥頭 .... 2 5 0 公克	250g(9oz.) .... red shallots	
冰糖 .... 3 大匙	3T. .... crystal sugar	

1 醬油、酒 ..... 各 2 大匙
1 •2T. each: soy sauce, cooking wine

2 水 .... 4 杯
醬油 .... ¹/₂ 杯
2 •4C. water
•¹/₂C. soy sauce

1 肋排洗淨，入**1**料醃 5 分鐘後，置平底鍋上煎至兩面呈金黃色，洋蔥洗淨切大塊，紅蔥頭洗淨切片備用。
2 鍋熱入油 5 大匙燒熱，入洋蔥、紅蔥頭爆香，續入**2**料煮開，再入肋排改小火燒煮 2 ¹/₂ 小時，最後入冰糖續煮 3 0 分鐘即可。

1 Wash the spare ribs, marinate in **1** for 5 minutes. In a flat frying pan, fry both sides until golden brown. Wash the onions, cut into large pieces. Wash the red shallots, cut into slices.
2 Heat the wok, add 5T. oil and heat. Fry the onions and red shallots until fragrant. Add **2** and bring to a boil; add the spare ribs, reduce to low heat, and simmer for 2¹/₂ hours. Stir in the crystal sugar and simmer for 30 minutes. Serve.

鹹菜炒豬肝
Sour Mustard Stick with Pork Liver

豬肝 .... 2 5 0 公克	250g(9oz.) .... pork liver	
鹹菜心 .... 1 0 0 公克	100g(3¹/₂oz.) ... sour mustard stick	
薑絲 .... 2 0 公克	20g(²/₃oz.) .. shredded ginger	
糖 .... 2 小匙	2t. .... sugar	

1 醬油、麻油 ... 各 1 大匙
1 •1T. each: soy sauce, sesame oil

1 豬肝洗淨切薄片，與**1**料拌勻醃 2 0 分鐘；鹹菜心洗淨切薄片備用。
2 鍋熱入油 3 杯燒至六分熱（ 1 4 0 ℃），入豬肝炸至變色，撈起備用。
3 鍋內留油 1 大匙，入薑絲爆香，續入鹹菜心及糖炒勻，再入豬肝拌勻即可。

1 Wash the pork liver, cut into thin slices, marinate with **1** for 20 minutes. Wash the sour mustard stick and cut into thin slices.
2 Heat the wok, add 3C. oil and heat to 140°C (280°F). Fry the liver quickly then remove.
3 Keep 1T. oil in the wok, fry the ginger until fragrant. Stir in the salted mustard stick and the sugar, fry thoroughly. Add the liver, mix well, and serve.

荷葉粉蒸肉
Steamed Pork in Lotus Wrappers

五花肉	3 0 0 公克	300g(10¹/₂oz.)	pork belly
蒸肉粉	4 包	4 packets	rice powder
荷葉	1 張	1 sheet	lotus leaf
高湯	¹/₂ 杯	¹/₂C.	stock

1
- 醬油 .... 3 大匙
- 紹興酒 .... 2 大匙

1
- •3T. soy sauce
- •2T. Chinese Shao-Shin wine

1 肉洗淨切 3×5 公分片狀，入 **1** 料醃 2 0 分鐘；荷葉泡軟洗淨備用。
2 五花肉入蒸肉粉拌勻，一片片置於荷葉上，再將剩餘蒸肉粉加入高湯拌勻，淋於肉上，入鍋蒸 1¹/₂ 小時即可。

1 Wash and cut the pork into 3 cm x 5 cm (1¹/₄"x2") slices, marinate in **1** for 20 minutes. Soak the lotus leaf until soft, then wash.
2 Mix the pork and rice powder well, arrange the pork slices one by one onto the lotus leaf. Mix the remaining rice powder with the stock well, pour over the pork, steam for 1¹/₂ hours.

芹菜牛肉絲
Shredded Beef with Celery

牛里肌	3 0 0 公克	300g(10¹/₂ oz.)	beef fillet
芹菜（淨重）	2 2 0 公克	220g(8oz., net weight)	celery
胡蘿蔔	7 0 公克	70g(2¹/₂ oz.)	carrots
薑絲	1 0 公克	10g(¹/₃ oz.) .	shredded ginger

1
- 醬油 .... 1¹/₃ 大匙
- 蠔油 .... 2 小匙
- 酒、太白粉 各 1 小匙
- 味精 .... ¹/₄ 小匙

1
- •1¹/₃ T. soy sauce
- •2t. oyster sauce
- •1t. each: cooking wine, cornstarch

2
- 酒 .... 2 小匙
- 糖、鹽 ... 各 ¹/₂ 小匙

2
- •2t. cooking wine
- •¹/₂ t. each: sugar, salt

1 牛肉逆紋切絲，入 **1** 料醃 3 0 分鐘，芹菜切 5 公分長段，胡蘿蔔切絲備用。
2 鍋熱入油¹/₂ 杯燒至六分熱（1 4 0℃），入牛肉炒至變色，隨即撈起瀝油，鍋內留油 2 大匙，入薑絲爆香，續入芹菜、胡蘿蔔略炒，最後再入牛肉及 **2** 料拌炒均勻即可。

1 Cut the beef against the grains into julienne strips, marinate in **1** for 30 minutes. Cut the celery into 5 cm (2") sections. Cut the carrots into julienne strips.
2 Heat the wok, add ¹/₂C. oil and heat to 140°C (280°F). Fry the beef until the color changes; remove from oil and drain. Keep 2T. oil in the wok and fry the shredded ginger until fragrant; mix in the celery and carrots, fry slightly. Add the beef and **2**, stir-fry thoroughly. Serve.

紅燒牛肉
Beef Stew

牛腩(圖1) ... 4 5 0 公克

1
蔥段 .... 4 段
薑片 .... 3 片
辣豆瓣醬 ..... 1 小匙
蒜末 .... $^1/_2$ 小匙

2
八角 .... 1 顆
花椒粒 ...... $^1/_2$ 小匙
小茴(圖2) .. $^1/_4$ 小匙
桂皮(拍碎) ... $^1/_8$ 小匙

3
水 .... 5 杯
醬油 .... 1 大匙
冰糖 .... 1 小匙
鹽 .... $^1/_4$ 小匙

450g(1lb.) ... beef brisket (Fig. 1)

1
- •4 sections green onion
- •3 slices ginger
- •1t. hot soy bean paste
- •$^1/_2$t. minced garlic

2
- •1 piece star anise
- •$^1/_2$t. Szechwan peppercorns
- •$^1/_4$t. fennel (Fig. 2)
- •$^1/_8$t. crushed cinnamon

3
- •5C. water
- •1T. soy sauce
- •1t. crystal sugar
- •$^1/_4$t. salt

1 牛腩洗淨，入開水中煮 1 分鐘後，隨即取出洗淨並切 3 公分塊狀。
2 **2**料裝入滷包袋（圖3）。
3 鍋熱入油 1 大匙燒熱，入**1**料爆香，續入牛腩炒香後，再入滷包袋、**3**料煮開，改小火煮 2 小時至湯汁濃稠即可。

1 Wash the beef, blanch in boiling water for 1 minute; remove, wash, and cut into 3 cm (1$^1/_4$") pieces.
2 Sew **2** into a small cloth bag (Fig. 3).
3 Heat the wok, add 1T. oil and heat. Fry **1** until fragrant, add the beef and stir-fry until fragrant. Add the cloth herb and **3**, bring to a boil; reduce to low heat and simmer until the sauce thickens (about 2 hours). Serve.

1

2

3

Shredded Beef with Green Peppers

牛里肌 ３００公克
青椒 ２００公克
蒜片 7公克
蔥段 .... 6 段
薑片 .... 6 片
紅辣椒 .... 2 條

1
水、油 各２大匙
醬油 .... 1 大匙
太白粉 .... 1 小匙
小蘇打 ......¹/₄ 小匙

2
水 ２大匙
酒 ２小匙
蠔油、醬油、麻油、太
白粉 各１小匙
糖、味精、胡椒粉 ...
..........各¹/₄小匙

300g(10¹/₂oz.) . beef fillet
200g(7oz.) .... green
peppers
7g(¹/₄oz.) ..... garlic slices
6 sections .. green onion
6 slices .... ginger
2 .... red chili pepper

1
•2T. each: water, oil
•1T. soy sauce
•1t. cornstarch
•¹/₄t. baking soda

2
•2T. water
•2t. cooking wine
•1t. each: oyster
sauce, soy sauce,
sesame oil,
cornstarch
•¹/₄t. each: sugar,
pepper

1 牛肉逆紋切薄片，入 **1** 料醃２０分鐘，青椒、紅辣椒去籽切片備用。
2 鍋熱入油¹/₂ 杯燒至五分熱（１２０℃），入牛肉炒至變色，隨即撈起瀝油。
3 鍋內留油２大匙燒熱，入紅辣椒片、蔥段、薑片、蒜片爆香，再入青椒炒至熟，隨即入牛肉及 **2**
料炒拌均勻即可。

1 Cut the beef against the grain into thin slices, marinate with **1** for 20 minutes. Discard the seeds in the green peppers and red chili pepper, slice.

2 Heat the wok, add ¹/₂C. oil and heat to 120°C (250°F). Stir-fry the beef until the color changes. Remove from oil and drain.

3 Keep 2T. oil in the wok and heat. Stir-fry the red chili pepper, green onions, ginger, and garlic until fragrant; add the green peppers and fry until cooked. Mix in the beef and **2**, stir-fry quickly. Serve.

蔥油香露雞
Green Onion Flavored Chicken

半土雞（1隻）..1500公克	1 (1500g or 3⅓lbs.) ....chicken
麻油 ....¼杯	¼C. ....sesame oil

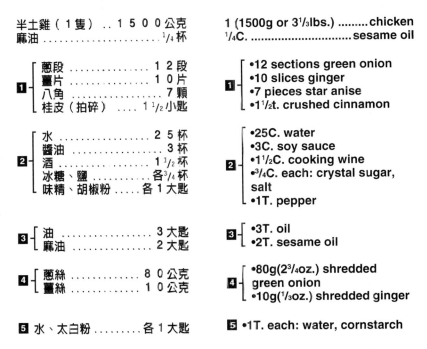

1
蔥段 ....1 2 段	•12 sections green onion
薑片 ....1 0 片	•10 slices ginger
八角 ....7 顆	•7 pieces star anise
桂皮（拍碎）....1 ½小匙	•1½t. crushed cinnamon

2
水 ....2 5 杯	•25C. water
醬油 ....3 杯	•3C. soy sauce
酒 ....1 ½杯	•1½C. cooking wine
冰糖、鹽 ....各¾杯	•¾C. each: crystal sugar, salt
味精、胡椒粉 .....各 1 大匙	•1T. pepper

3
油 ....3 大匙	•3T. oil
麻油 ....2 大匙	•2T. sesame oil

4
蔥絲 ....8 0 公克	•80g(2¾oz.) shredded green onion
薑絲 ....1 0 公克	•10g(⅓oz.) shredded ginger

5 水、太白粉 ....各 1 大匙   **5** •1T. each: water, cornstarch

1 雞洗淨，去雞爪。
2 取一深鍋燒熱，入油 2 大匙燒熱，入**1**料爆香，續入**2**料煮開，蓋上鍋蓋以小火煮 3 0 分鐘，再將雞放入續煮 1 0 分鐘，熄火浸泡 1 0 分鐘（雞必須完全浸泡在滷汁中）。
3 將泡熟的雞取出，滷汁留用，表面塗抹一層麻油後吊起，待雞冷卻後切塊、排盤。
4 鍋熱入**3**料燒熱，入**4**料爆香，續入滷汁 2 杯煮開，再以**5**料芶芡，淋在雞塊上即可。

1 Wash the chicken and cut off the chicken feet.
2 Heat a deep skillet, add 2T. oil and heat. Stir-fry **1** until fragrant, then add **2** and bring to a boil. Cover with lid and simmer over low heat for 30 minutes. Add the chicken to the skillet and cook for 10 minutes. Turn off the heat and soak the chicken for 10 minutes (sauce must cover the chicken).
3 Remove the cooked chicken from skillet, brush the whole chicken with sesame oil; hang until cool. Chop the chicken into serving pieces and arrange on a dish. Keep the sauce for later use.
4 Add **3** to a pre-heated wok and stir-fry **4** until fragrant. Add 2C. of the sauce and bring to a boil; thicken with **5** . Pour over the chicken and serve.

芋艿雞骨醬
Taro with Chicken

雞腿 .... 5 5 0 公克
小芋艿（圖 1） 3 0 0 公克
醬油露 .... 3 大匙

1
- 蔥段 .... 5 段
- 薑片 .... 5 片

2
- 水 .... 3 杯
- 醬油露 ...... 2 大匙
- 冰糖 ...... 1 1/2 大匙
- 紹興酒 .... 1 大匙

550g(1¼lbs.) ..... chicken legs
300g(10½oz.) .... baby taros (Fig. 1)
3T. .... soy sauce

1
- •5 sections green onion
- •5 slices ginger

2
- •3C. water
- •2T. soy sauce
- •1½T. crystal sugar
- •1T. Chinese Shao-Shin wine

1 小芋艿洗淨、去皮，入蒸鍋蒸 4 0 分鐘備用。
2 雞腿洗淨、去皮，切 3 × 2 公分塊狀。
3 鍋熱入油 3 大匙燒熱，入 **1** 料炒香，續入雞塊與醬油露炒片刻，再入 **2** 料以小火煮 4 0 分鐘，最後入芋艿，並開大火將湯汁收乾即可。
■ 小芋艿因生產季節有限，可以芋頭去皮切塊代替。

1 Wash and pare the taros. Steam for 40 minutes.
2 Wash and remove the skin from the chicken legs, cut into 3 cm x 2 cm (1¼"x1") pieces.
3 Preheat the wok, add 3T. oil and heat. Stir-fry **1** until fragrant. Stir in the chicken and the soy sauce, fry slightly; add **2** and cook over low heat for 40 minutes. Add the taros and cook over high heat until sauce evaporates. Serve.
■ The harvest season of the baby taros is limited. Baby taros may be substituted with regular size taros pared and cut into serving pieces.

1

雞（半隻）... 5 5 0 公克
栗子（圖 1 ） 1 5 0 公克
醬油露 .... 4 大匙
糖 .... 1 小匙

1
蔥段 .... 5 段
薑片 .... 5 片

2
水 .... 4 杯
醬油露 ...... 1 大匙
冰糖 .... 1 小匙
味精 .... $1/8$ 小匙

550g(1¼lbs.) ..... chicken
150g(5¼oz.) .. chestnuts
(Fig. 1)
4T. .... soy sauce
1t. .... sugar

1
•5 sections green
onion
•5 slices ginger

2
•4C. water
•1T. soy sauce
•1t. crystal sugar

1 雞洗淨切 4 × 3 公分塊狀，以醬油露 1 大匙醃 1 0 分鐘。栗子洗淨泡水 1 小時，以牙籤挑去殘留外殼後，加水 1 杯蒸 2 0 分鐘，再加糖 1 小匙蒸 1 0 分鐘，取出瀝乾備用。
2 鍋熱入油 3 大匙燒熱，入 **1** 料炒香，再入雞塊與 3 大匙醬油露炒至變色，隨入 **2** 料小火燒煮 2 0 分鐘，取出蔥段、薑片，再入栗子小火煮 4 0 分鐘後，改大火將湯汁收乾即可。（燒煮時不使用鍋鏟，只需搖動炒鍋，以免栗子碎裂。）

1 Wash the chicken and cut into 4 cm x 3 cm (1½"x1¼") pieces. Marinate the chicken with 1T. soy sauce for 10 minutes. Wash the chestnuts and soak in water for 1 hour; use a toothpick to peel off the skin. Steam the chestnuts with 1C. water for 20 minutes, add 1t. sugar and steam for 10 more minutes. Drain.
2 Preheat the wok, add 3T. oil and heat. Stir-fry **1** until fragrant. Stir in the chicken and 3T. soy sauce; fry until color changes. Add **2** and simmer over low heat for 20 minutes. Discard the green onions and ginger from the wok; add the chestnuts and simmer over low heat for 40 minutes. Turn heat to high and cook until sauce is reduced to ½C. To avoid breaking the chestunts, do not stir with spatula; shake the wok when necessary. Serve.

1

木耳子雞
Chicken with Wood Ears

雞腿 550公克
薄濕木耳（圖1） ....
.... 200公克
薑 50公克
蔥段 5段

1
水 .... 2 大匙
太白粉 ..... 1 ½ 大匙
鹽 .... ½ 小匙

2
水 .... 2 杯
酒 .... 1 小匙
鹽 .... ¾ 小匙
糖 .... ¼ 小匙
胡椒粉、味精各 ⅛ 小匙

550g(1⅕lbs.) ..... chicken legs
200g(7oz.) .... soaked wood ears (Fig. 1)
50g(1¾oz.) .... ginger
5 sections .. green onion

1
•2T. water
•1½T. cornstarch
•½t. salt

2
•2C. water
•1t. cooking wine
•¾t. salt
•¼t. sugar
•⅛t. pepper

1 雞腿洗淨切 2 × 1 公分塊狀，入 **1** 料醃 1 0 分鐘；薑洗淨切片，木耳洗淨去蒂（圖 2），用手撕成 3 × 2 公分片狀備用。
2 鍋熱入油 3 大匙燒熱，入薑片炒香(約 1 分鐘)，續入雞肉與蔥段炒熟，再入木耳與 **2** 料煮開，改中火續煮 5 分鐘即可。

1 Wash the chicken and cut into 2 cm x 1 cm (1"x½") pieces. Marinate the chicken with **1** for 10 minutes. Cut the ginger into thin slices. Wash the wood ears, discard the stems (illus. 2), and tear into 3cm x 2 cm (1¼"x1") slices.
2 Heat the wok, add 3T. oil and heat. Stir-fry the ginger until fragrant (about 1 minute). Stir in the chicken and green onions; fry until cooked. Add the wood ears and **2**, bring to a boil. Reduce to medium heat and cook for 5 minutes. Serve.

1

2

Stir-fried Chicken Fillets with Gee-Tsai

雞胸肉 300公克
薺菜 150公克

1
- 蛋白 .... 1 個
- 水 .... 1 大匙
- 太白粉 .... 1 小匙
- 麻油 .... ¹/₂ 小匙
- 鹽 .... ¹/₃ 小匙
- 胡椒粉 ...... ¹/₈ 小匙

2
- 水 .... ¹/₂ 杯
- 太白粉、麻油、酒 ...
　　......... 各¹/₂ 小匙
- 鹽 .... ¹/₄ 小匙
- 胡椒粉、味精各¹/₈ 小匙

300g(10¹/₂oz.) ....chicken breast
150g(5¹/₄oz.) ......gee-tsai (Chinese cress)

1
- •1 egg white
- •1T. water
- •1t. cornstarch
- •¹/₂t. sesame oil
- •¹/₃t. salt
- •¹/₈t. pepper

2
- •¹/₂C. water
- •¹/₂t. each: sesame oil, cornstarch, cooking wine
- •¹/₄t. salt
- •¹/₈t. pepper

1

1 雞胸肉洗淨，切3×2公分薄片，以 **1** 料醃10分鐘。
2 薺菜洗淨、切末，入開水中再煮開，取出漂涼，擠乾水份備用。
3 鍋熱入油¹/₂杯燒熱，入雞片炒至變色，撈起瀝乾。
4 鍋內留油3大匙，入薺菜炒香，續入雞片與 **2** 料炒拌均勻即可。
■ 薺菜因時節與地區不同，不易購買時，可以西洋菜（圖1）代替。
■ 雪菜雞片：將薺菜改為雪裡紅100公克，其餘材料及作法與薺菜雞片相同。

1 Wash the chicken breast; cut into 3 cm x 2 cm (1¹/₄"x1") slices. Marinate in **1** for 10 minutes.
2 Wash and mince the gee-tsai. Blanch in boiling water; rinse under cold water. Squeeze out the water.
3 Preheat a wok; add ¹/₂C. oil and heat. Stir-fry the chicken until color changes, remove and drain.
4 Keep 3T. oil in the wok. Fry the gee-tsai until fragrant; stir in the chicken and **2** ; mix well. Serve.
■ Gee-tsai may be substituted with watercress (Fig. 1)
■ Mustard Green with Chicken: Replace gee-tsai with 100g(3¹/₂oz.) of salted mustard green. The rest of the ingredients and the cooking methods are the same as above.

砂鍋油豆腐雞
Braised Chicken and Fried Tofu in Ceramic Pot

雞腿 ４５０公克
油豆腐（６塊）（圖１）．
.... １００公克
粉絲（１把）... ４０公克
蔥末 １大匙

1 蔥段 ５段
薑片 ３片

2 醬油 ４大匙
酒 １大匙
冰糖 １小匙

3 熱水 ２杯
小蘇打 １小匙

450g(1lb.)..chicken legs
100g(3½oz., 6 cakes) ....
fried tofu (Fig. 1)
1 bunch (40g or 1½oz) ..
bean thread
1T..minced green onion

1 •5 sections green
onion
•3 slices ginger

2 •4T. soy sauce
•1T. cooking wine
•1t. crystal sugar

3 •2C. hot water
•1t. baking soda

1 油豆腐以**3**料浸泡５分鐘取出，沖洗乾淨後擠乾備用。粉絲入溫水中泡軟（約５分鐘），取出瀝乾，切成３公分長段，雞腿洗淨切塊。
2 砂鍋燒熱入油１大匙燒熱，入**1**料爆香，再入雞塊炒熟，隨即入**2**料將雞肉炒至上色，再入水４杯煮開後，續煮２０分鐘，入油豆腐再煮５分鐘，最後入粉絲煮開，再灑上蔥末即可。

1 Soak the fried tofu in **3** for 5 minutes, remove; rinse and squeeze out the water. Soak the bean thread in warm water (about 5 minutes) to soften, drain. Cut the bean thread into 3 cm (1¼ ") sections. Wash the chicken legs, cut into serving size pieces.
2 Heat a ceramic pot, add 1T. oil and heat. Stir-fry **1** until fragrant, add the chicken and fry until cooked. Mix in **2** and stir until the chicken pieces are well coated with soy sauce. Add 4C. water and bring to a boil. Reduce the heat and cook for another 20 minutes. Add the tofu and cook for 5 minutes; add the bean threads and bring to a boil. Sprinkle with minced green onion before serving.

1

雞腿（2隻）	600公克	600g(1⅓lbs.) ...chicken legs

1
蔥段 .... 12 段
薑片 .... 5 片
鹽 .... 2 大匙

1
• 12 sections green onion
• 5 slices ginger
• 2T. salt

2
紹興酒 .... 1 杯
蝦油 .... 2 大匙
鹽、胡椒粉 各 ¼ 小匙

2
• 1C. Chinese shao-shin wine
• 2T. shrimp oil
• ¼t. each: salt, pepper

1 雞腿洗淨，以 **1** 料抹勻醃 1 5 分鐘。水 7 杯煮開，將醃好的雞腿入鍋煮 1 0 分鐘後，熄火浸泡 1 5 分鐘，取雞湯 3 杯待涼備用。
2 取一容器，將雞腿、**2** 料及雞湯放入（湯汁須蓋過雞腿），蓋上保鮮膜入冰箱冷藏，隔日取出切塊即可。

1 Wash the chicken legs, marinate in **1** for 15 minutes. Bring 7C. water to a boil in a pot, add the marinated chicken legs. Cook for 10 minutes, remove from heat and soak for 15 minutes. Remove the chicken legs. Keep 3C. chicken broth; cool for later use.
2 Place the chicken legs in a deep container. Pour **2** and 3C. chicken broth over chicken (must cover the chicken legs). Cover with cellophane paper and keep in refrigerator overnight. Cut into serving pieces the next day. Serve cold.

醬爆雞丁
Stir-fried Chicken in Bean Paste Sauce
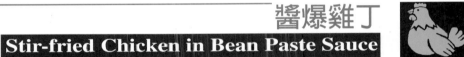

雞腿（2隻）	600公克	2(600g or 1⅓lbs.) ....chicken legs
熟毛豆仁	80公克	80g(2¾oz.)boiled soy beans
蒜片	10片	10 slices ....garlic

1
蛋白 .... 1 個
太白粉 .... 1 小匙
鹽 .... ¼ 小匙
胡椒粉 .... ⅛ 小匙

1
• 1 egg white
• 1t. cornstarch
• ¼t. salt
• ⅛t. pepper

2
甜麵醬、水 各 2 大匙
糖 .... ½ 大匙
麻油 .... 1 小匙

2
• 2T. each: water, sweet soy bean paste
• ½T. sugar
• 1t. sesame oil

1 雞腿洗淨去骨，切 1×1 公分小丁，以 **1** 料醃 1 0 分鐘。鍋熱入油½ 杯燒熱，入雞丁炒至熟，取出瀝油備用。
2 鍋內留油 1 小匙，入蒜片爆香，續入 **2** 料炒香，再入雞丁與毛豆仁拌炒均勻即可。

1 Remove the bones from the chicken legs, wash and cut into 1 cm x 1 cm (½"x½") pieces. Marinate with **1** for 10 minutes. Heat the wok, add ½C. oil and heat. Stir-fry the chicken pieces until cooked; remove from oil and drain.
2 Keep 1t. oil in the wok and stir-fry the garlic slices until fragrant. Mix in **2** and fry until fragrant. Add the chicken pieces and soy beans, mix well. Serve.

杭州醬鴨
Hangchow Marinated Duck

鴨（1隻）...... 1 8 0 0公克	1 (1800g or 4 lbs.) ....duck
淺色醬油 .... 4 杯	4C. ....light soy sauce
鹽 .... 2 大匙	2T. ....salt
紹興酒 .... 1 大匙	1T. ....Chinese Shao-Shin wine
糖 .... ¹/₂大匙	¹/₂T. ....sugar
蔥段 .... 3 段	3 sections ....green onion
薑片 .... 2 片	2 slices ....ginger
硝 .... 0 . 1 8公克	0.18g ....sodium nitrite

1 鴨洗淨去鴨掌，用小鐵鉤勾住鴨鼻孔（圖1），掛在通風處風乾水份（約2小時）。

2 將鹽和硝拌勻，在鴨身內外抹勻後，將鴨頭扭向胸前挾在右腋下（圖2），平整地放進長方形保鮮盒內，蓋好放入冰箱冷藏醃 1¹/₂天後，翻身再醃 1¹/₂天即可取出，倒掉汁液。

3 鴨再放入保鮮盒內入醬油浸泡，蓋好再放入冰箱冷藏浸泡 2 天後，翻身再浸泡 2 天取出，腹部剖開，再用兩支竹筷子，從腹部刀口處塞入肚內，使腹腔向兩側敞開（圖3）。

4 將醃鴨的醬油倒入鍋中煮開，入鴨並月湯杓將醬油徐徐淋在鴨身上至呈暗紅色撈起，置通風處風乾 2 天。

5 醬鴨放在大盤子上，灑上糖、蔥段、薑片及紹興酒，入鍋大火蒸 2 0 分鐘，冷卻後切塊裝盤即可。

■ 由於硝用量受限制，且量太少不易秤量，因此建議讀者取硝¹/₄小匙分成 7 等份，取其中 1 份即為 1 隻鴨的硝用量。

1 Wash the duck and cut off the duck feet. Hang the duck (Fig. 1) from an iron hook, and air-dry for about 2 hours.

2 Mix the salt and sodium nitrite well, rub the inside and the outside of the duck with the mixture. Twist the duck head under the right wing (Fig. 2). Place the duck in an air-tight container, cover, and refrigerate for 1¹/₂ days. Turn the duck and marinate for another 1¹/₂ days. Remove; discard the liquid.

3 Soak the duck in the soy sauce in an air tight container. Refrigerate for 2 more days; turn the duck and soak for another 2 days; remove. Cut open the cavity of the duck, insert a pair of bamboo chopsticks in the cavity and split open into two halves (Fig. 3).

4 Bring the soy sauce for marinating the duck to a boil. Add the duck and spoon sauce onto duck constantly until the color turns dark red. Remove and air-dry for 2 days.

5 Place the duck on a big plate; sprinkle with sugar, green onions, ginger, and Chinese Shao-Shin wine. Steam over high heat for 20 minutes. Cool and cut into serving pieces. Arrange on a plate and serve.

■ Sodium nitrite should be used at a minimum. Divide ¹/₄t. sodium nitrite into 7 equal portions. Use one portion for one duck.

1

2

3

紅燒八寶鴨
Braised Soy Duck with Eight Treasures

鴨（1隻） 1800公克
香菇 5公克
圓糯米 .... ³/₄杯
醬油 3大匙

1
瘦肉、鴨肫、中式火腿
、熟筍、蓮子 ....
.... 各30公克
栗子、青豆仁 ....
.... 各20公克

2
水 ....¹/₂杯
醬油 1¹/₂大匙
酒、麻油 ... 各1小匙
胡椒粉 ......¹/₃小匙

3
醬油 ....¹/₂杯
酒 1大匙
冰糖 1小匙
蔥段 5段
薑片 5片

1 (1800g or 4lbs.) ..duck
5g(¹/₆oz.) ......dried black
mushrooms
³/₄C. ....short grain
glutinous rice
3T. ....soy sauce

1
•30g(1oz.) each: lean
pork, duck gizzard,
Chinese ham, boiled
bamboo shoots,
lotus seeds
•20g(²/₃oz.) each:
chestnuts, green
peas

2
•¹/₂C. water
•1¹/₂T. soy sauce
•1t. each: cooking
wine, sesame oil
•¹/₃t. pepper

3
•¹/₂C. soy sauce
•1T. cooking wine
•1t. crystal sugar
•5 sections green
onion
•5 slices ginger

1 圓糯米洗淨泡水1小時瀝乾，再加水¹/₂杯煮成糯米飯，栗子、蓮子洗淨加水1杯蒸熟，中式火腿亦蒸熟備用。
2 香菇泡軟去蒂，與瘦肉、鴨肫、中式火腿、筍均切1公分立方小丁備用。
3 鍋熱入油1大匙燒熱，入香菇炒香，續入**1**料炒熟，再入**2**料煮開後，入糯米飯拌炒均勻即為八寶料，將八寶料塞入鴨肚內，缺口用針線縫緊（參考52頁）。
4 鴨身抹上醬油，入九分熱（200℃）油鍋中，大火炸至金黃色，撈起瀝油備用。
5 水16杯煮開，入鴨及**3**料再煮開，蓋鍋蓋改小火續煮至鴨肉熟爛（約4小時，其間須翻轉鴨身數次），取出盛盤，餘汁續煮到剩1杯，淋在鴨上即可。

1 Wash and soak the short grain glutinous rice in water for 1 hour, drain; add ¹/₂C. water and cook the rice. Wash the chestnuts and the lotus seeds, add 1C. water and steam until cooked. Steam the ham until cooked.
2 Soak the mushrooms until soft, discard the stems. Cut the mushrooms, lean pork, duck gizzard, ham, and bamboo shoots into 1 cm (¹/₂") cubes.
3 Heat the wok, add 1T. oil and heat. Stir-fry the mushrooms until fragrant. Add **1** and fry until cooked. Stir in **2** and bring to a boil; add the glutinous rice, then stir-fry and mix well. Stuff the filling into the cavity of the duck, sew the opening shut (see p-52).
4 Brush the duck with soy sauce. Heat the wok, add oil and heat to 200°C (390°F). Deep-fry the duck over high heat until golden brown; remove and drain.
5 Bring 16C. water to a boil. Add the duck and **3** and bring to a boil again. Cover, reduce to low heat, and simmer until duck is well done (about 4 hours, turn the duck several times). Remove the duck and arrange on a plate. Cook the sauce until the liquid is reduced to about 1C.; pour the sauce over the duck. Serve.

鴨（1隻）　1800公克
麵粉 . . . . 1/2 杯
花椒粒（圖1）、鹽、酒 .
. . . . 各2大匙
蔥段 10段
薑片 5片
蛋白 1個

1(1800g or 4 lbs.) ..duck
1/2C. ....flour
2T. each: ....Szechwan
peppercorns (Fig. 1),
salt, cooking wine
10 sections green onion
5 slices ....ginger
1 ....egg white

1 花椒粒入鍋小火炒至香味出來，再入鹽同炒1分鐘，取出待涼後，入拍碎之蔥段（圖2）、薑片與酒拌勻。
2 鴨洗淨擦乾水份，以1項材料在鴨身內、外抹勻，並置冰箱內冷藏6小時至入味。
3 鴨入蒸鍋大火蒸至鴨肉熟爛（約2 1/2 小時），取出去掉蔥、薑，待涼備用。
4 鴨身抹上蛋白，再沾上麵粉，入九分熱（200℃）油鍋中，大火炸至金黃色即可。
■ 食時可沾椒鹽，並配以白饅頭。

1

2

1 Stir-fry the Szechwan peppercorns over low heat until fragrant; add the salt and fry for 1 minute; remove and cool. Add the smashed green onions (Fig. 2), ginger, and cooking wine. Mix well.
2 Wash the duck and pat dry. Rub the inside and outside of the duck with step 1 ingredients, refrigerate for 6 hours until the flavor permeates.
3 Steam the duck over high heat until well done (about 2 1/2 hours); discard the green onions and ginger; remove and cool.
4 Brush the duck with egg white, then dust with flour. Heat the wok, add oil and heat to 200°C (390°F). Deep-fry the duck over high heat until golden brown. Serve.
■ Duck may be served with Szechwan pepper salt and steamed buns.

清蒸八寶鴨
Steamed Duck with Eight Treasures

鴨（1隻） 1700公克
覆菜葉......... 30公克
圓糯米 ....³/₄杯
鹽 1大匙

1
水 2杯
酒、麻油、鹽、醬油.
............各1小匙
糖 .... ¹/₄小匙
味精、胡椒粉各¹/₈小匙

2
瘦肉、鴨肫、鴨肝、鴨
心、筍 ...各30公克
香菇 10公克
白果 8個

3
中式火腿 ... 50公克
薑片 9片
蔥段 9段

1 (1700g or 3³/₄lbs.)duck
30g(1oz.) ..fu tsia leaves
³/₄C. ....short grain
glutinous rice
1T. ....salt

1
•2C. water
•1t. each: cooking
wine, sesame oil,
salt, soy sauce
•¹/₄t. sugar
•¹/₈t. pepper

2
•30g(1oz.)each: lean
pork, duck gizzard,
duck liver, bamboo
shoots, duck heart
•10g(¹/₃oz.) dried
black mushrooms
•8 gingko nuts

3
•50g(1³/₄oz.) Chinese
ham
•9 slices ginger
•9 sections green
onion

1 鴨洗淨瀝乾，在鴨身內外抹鹽，醃1小時備用。
2 **2**料洗淨，除白果外均切小丁，中式火腿洗淨切片。
3 圓糯米洗淨泡水3小時，瀝乾水份，與**1**、**2**料拌勻入鍋炒5分鐘，待涼塞入鴨腹中，缺口用針線縫緊（圖1），置於蒸盤中，再將**3**料平均地排在鴨身上（圖2），最後將覆菜葉完整地覆蓋鴨身（圖3），入鍋蒸5小時即可。

1 Wash and drain the duck; rub the salt inside and outside the duck. Marinate for 1 hour.
2 Wash **2**, cut all ingredients into cubes except the gingko nuts. Wash and slice the ham.
3 Wash and soak the short grain glutinous rice in water for 3 hours, drain. Mix **1** and **2** well, stir-fry for 5 minutes. Cool the stir-fry mixture, then put into the cavity of the duck. Sew the opening shut (Fig. 1). Place the duck on a steam plate, arrange **3** on the duck (Fig. 2). Cover the duck with fu tsai leaves (Fig. 3), and steam for 5 hours. Serve.

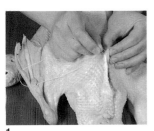

1

2

3

Salted Duck with Osmanthus Flavor

鴨（1隻）　1700公克
鹽 500公克
八角（圖1）... 30公克
桂花醬（圖2）... 1大匙
花椒粒 .... ½大匙

1
紹興酒 1大匙
蔥段 8段
薑片 5片

1 (1700g or 3¾lbs.)duck
500g(1lb.) .... salt
30g(1oz.) ...... star anises
(Fig. 1)
1T. ....osmanthus jam
(Fig. 2)
½T. ....Szechwan
peppercorns

1
•1T.Chinese Sho-
Shin wine
•8 sections green
onion
•5 slices ginger

1 鴨洗淨瀝乾水份，用叉子在鴨身上叉洞（圖3），以利調跌汁之滲入。
2 鍋熱入花椒粒小火炒30秒，再入鹽、八角、**1**料和水30杯煮40分鐘為白滷汁。
3 將鴨入白滷汁中煮5分鐘，再入桂花醬熄火浸泡24小時（鴨身必須完全浸泡滷汁中），最後取出切塊即可。

1 Wash and pat dry the duck. Use fork to poke holes in the duck (Fig. 3).
2 Heat the wok, fry the Szechwan peppercorns over low heat for 30 seconds. Add the salt, star anises, **1**, and 30C. water; cook for 40 minutes to make the brine.
3 Cook the duck in the brine for 5 minutes. Stir in the osmanthus jam, remove from heat, and soak in the brine for 24 hours (duck must be covered by the brine). Remove, cut into pieces and serve cold.

1

2

3

煙燻素鵝
Smoked Vegetarian Rolls

熟筍	7 0 公克	70g(2¹/₂oz.) .... boiled or canned bamboo shoots	
胡蘿蔔	6 0 公克	60g(2oz.) .... carrot	
香菇	1 0 公克	10g(¹/₃oz.) .... dried black mushrooms	
豆皮	8 張	8 pieces .... bean curd skin	
薑末	1 大匙	1T. .... minced ginger	

1
水	¹/₂ 杯
鹽	¹/₂ 小匙
味精	¹/₄ 小匙

1
- ¹/₂C. water
- ¹/₂t. salt

2
水	1 小匙
太白粉	¹/₂ 小匙

2
- 1t. water
- ¹/₂t. cornstarch

3
水	3 杯
麻油、糖	各 2 大匙
鹽	¹/₂ 大匙
味精	¹/₄ 小匙

3
- 3C. water
- 2T. each: sesame oil, sugar
- ¹/₂T. salt

4
茶葉、糖	各 2 大匙
米	1 大匙

4
- 2T. each: tea leaves, sugar
- 1T. rice

1 胡蘿蔔去皮洗淨，香菇泡軟去蒂，與熟筍均切絲備用。
2 鍋熱入油 3 大匙燒熱，入薑末、香菇爆香，續入胡蘿蔔、筍拌炒均勻，再入**1**料拌炒至入味後，以**2**料勾芡即為內餡。分成 2 等份。
3 **3**料拌勻，將豆反放入**3**料中浸濕，取此交錯疊四張（圖 1 ）共 2 份，將 1 份餡置 1 份皮中（圖 2 ），再捲起並以牙籤固定（圖 3 ）共兩捲，入鍋蒸 6 分鐘取出待涼，即為素鵝。
4 另鍋入**4**料，上置架子，素鵝置架子上，蓋上鍋蓋用小火燻至上色（約 8 分鐘）即可。

1 Wash and peel the carrot; soak the mushrooms until soft, discard the stems; cut carrot, mushrooms, and bamboo shoots into julienne strips.
2 To make the filling: Heat the wok, add 3T. oil and heat. Fry the ginger and the mushrooms until fragrant. Add the carrot and bamboo shoots, mix well. Stir in **1** and stir-fry until tasty. Thicken with **2**, divide into 2 equal portions.
3 Wet the bean curd skins with well-mixed **3**; separate into 2 portions of four each. Lay each portion of bean curd skins one by one on alternate sides (Fig. 1). Put the filling on each bean curd sheet (Fig. 2), roll into a cylinder and close with toothpicks (Fig. 3) Steam for six minutes, remove and cool.
4 Place **4** in another pot, put a rack over, and place the "Vegetarian Rolls" on the rack; cover the wok tightly and smoke over low heat until light brown (about 8 minutes). Serve.

1

2

3

紅燒豆腐
Braised Soy Tofu

絞肉............ ６０公克
胡蘿蔔、濕木耳各４０公克
熟筍............ ３０公克
香菇............. ５公克
蔥段............. ５段
豆腐............ １½塊

1
高湯 ....¹/₂杯
醬油 ....¹/₂大匙
糖 ....¹/₂小匙

2
高湯 ....¹/₂杯
醬油 １¹/₂大匙
醬色、酒、麻油 .....
.... 各１大匙
糖 ....¹/₂小匙
味精 ....¹/₄小匙

3
水 １小匙
太白粉 ....¹/₂小匙

60g(2oz.) ...ground pork
40g(1¹/₃oz.) each: ....
carrot, soaked wood
ears
30g(1oz.) ....boiled or
canned bamboo shoots
5g(¹/₆oz.) ......dried black
mushrooms
5 sections ..green onion
1¹/₂ pieces .....bean curd
(Tofu)

1
•¹/₂C. stock
•¹/₂T. soy sauce
•¹/₂t. sugar

2
•¹/₂C. stock
•1¹/₂T. soy sauce
•1T. each: soy sauce
coloring, cooking
wine, sesame oil
•¹/₂t. sugar

3
•1t. water
•¹/₂t. cornstarch

1 香菇泡軟去蒂洗淨切半，木耳去蒂，與熟筍、胡蘿蔔均切３×３公分片狀，豆腐切５×３公分片狀備用。
2 鍋熱入油３杯燒至八分熱（約１８０℃），入豆腐炸至金黃色，撈起瀝油備用。
3 另鍋熱入油２大匙燒熱，入蔥段、香菇爆香，續入絞肉、胡蘿蔔、筍、木耳及**1**料，改小火慢煮１０分鐘，再入豆腐及**2**料煮至入味後，以**3**料芶芡即可。

1 Soak the mushrooms, discard the stems, cut in half; discard the stems of the wood ears. Cut mushrooms, wood ears, carrot, and boiled bamboo shoots into 3 cm x 3 cm (1¹/₄"x 1¹/₄") slices. Cut the bean curd into 5 cm x 3 cm (2"x1¹/₄") slices.
2 Heat the wok, add 3C. oil and heat to 180°C (360°F). Deep-fry the bean curd until golden brown; remove and drain.
3 Heat the wok, add 2T. oil and heat. Fry the green onions and the mushrooms until fragrant. Mix in the ground pork, carrot, bamboo shoots, wood ears, and **1**; reduce to low heat and simmer for 10 minutes. Add the bean curd and **2**, cook until the flavor penetrated the bean curd; thicken with **3**, and serve.

56

麵筋泡 .... 1 5 0 公克
胡蘿蔔 .... 5 0 公克
熟毛豆仁（圖 1） 3 0 公克
香菇 .... 1 0 公克
蔥末 .... 2 大匙

1
高湯 ....¹/₂ 杯
醬油 ....¹/₂ 大匙
糖 ....¹/₂ 小匙
味精 ....¹/₈ 小匙

2
糖色、醬油　各 1 大匙
麻油、糖 ...各 1 小匙
味精 ....¹/₈ 小匙

150g(5¹/₄oz.) ....wheat gluten puffs
50g(1³/₄oz.) ....carrot
30g(1oz.) ....boiled fresh soy beans (Fig. 1)
10g(¹/₃oz.) ....dried black mushrooms
2T.minced green onion

1
•¹/₂C. stock
•¹/₂T. soy sauce
•¹/₂t. sugar

2
•1T. each: sugar coloring, soy sauce
•1t. each: sesame oil, sugar

1 麵筋泡以熱水泡軟（圖 2）：再以冷水洗去大部份的油脂後瀝乾，胡蘿蔔切 2 × 3 公分薄片，香菇泡軟去蒂切半。
2 鍋熱入油 1 大匙燒熱，入香菇爆香後，續入蔥末炒勻，再入**1**料及胡蘿蔔改小火煮 1 0 分鐘後，加入麵筋泡及**2**料拌炒至湯汁快收乾時，入毛豆仁拌勻即可。

1 Soak the wheat gluten puffs in hot water until soft (Fig. 2); wash in cold water to remove most of the grease, drain. Cut the carrot into 2 cm x 3 cm (1"x1¹/₄") slices. Soak the mushrooms until soft, discard the stems, cut in half.
2 Heat the wok, add 1T. oil and heat. Fry the mushrooms until fragrant, add the green onions and stir-fry. Mix in **1** and the carrot, reduce to low heat and simmer for 10 minutes. Stir in the wheat gluten puffs and **2** stir until sauce is almost evaporated; add the soy beans and stir-fry evenly. Serve.

1

2

素雞
Vegetarian Chicken Rolls

豆包 .... 3 7 5 公克
豆皮 .... 2 張
棉繩 .... 2 條

1
麻油 .... 2 ½ 大匙
鹽 ....²/₃ 大匙
味精 .... ½ 小匙
蛋 .... 1 ½ 個

375g(13¼oz.) ....bean curd pockets
2 sheets bean curd skin
2 pieces ....cotton string

1
• 2½T. sesame oil
• ²/₃T. salt
• 1½ eggs

1 豆包一張張拆開（圖1），入**1**料醃2－3小時至入味，分成2等份。
2 豆皮攤開，上置醃好的豆包，捲成圓筒狀並壓緊，外面用玻璃紙包起來（圖2），最外層再用紗布包緊並用棉繩捆緊（圖3），入鍋蒸1小時，取出待涼，拆開棉繩、紗布、玻璃紙再切片即可。

1 Open the bean curd pockets one by one (Fig. 1); marinate in **1** for 2-3 hours, divide into 2 portions.
2 Spread open the bean curd skins, place the marinated bean curd pockets on the bean curd skin; roll into cylinders and press tight. Wrap with cellophane paper (Fig. 2); then wrap with a cheese cloth. Tightly tie the roll with a cotton string (Fig. 3). Steam for 1 hour, cool; remove the cotton string, cloth, and cellophane paper. Slice and serve.

1

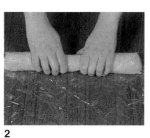

2

3

黃豆芽（圖1）400公克
油炸豆包 80公克
青蒜 1枝
紅辣椒 1條
薑片 1片

1
水 1¹/₂杯
醬油 2大匙
冰糖 2小匙
花椒粒、小茴各¹/₄小匙
甘草（圖2）... 1片

2
麻油、黑醋　各1小匙
味精 ....¹/₈小匙

400g(14oz.) ..... soy bean sprouts (Fig. 1)
80g(2³/₄oz.) .... fried bean curd pockets
1 stalk .... garlic leek
1 .... red chili pepper
1 slice .... ginger

1
•1¹/₂C. water
•2T. soy sauce
•2t. crystal sugar
•¹/₄t. each: fennels, Szechwan peppercorns
•1 piece licorice (Fig. 2)

2
•1t. each: sesame oil, brown vinegar

1 黃豆芽洗淨入鍋燙熟，隨即撈起瀝乾，豆包切絲，青蒜、紅辣椒洗淨切斜片備用。
2 鍋熱入油2大匙燒熱，入青蒜、辣椒及薑片爆香，續入**1**料煮開，改小火煮至湯汁剩¹/₂杯（30分鐘），撈去殘渣後，再入黃豆芽及豆包拌炒勻隨即盛起，待涼，入**2**料拌勻即可。

1 Wash the soy bean sprouts, scald quickly in boiling water, remove and drain. Cut the fried bean curd pockets into julienne strips; wash the garlic leek and the red chili pepper, cut both into slanted slices.
2 Heat the wok, add 2T. oil and heat. Stir-fry the garlic leek, red chili pepper, and ginger until fragrant. Add **1** and bring to a boil, reduce to low heat and simmer until the sauce reduces to ¹/₂C. (about 30 minutes). Strain the sauce and return the sauce to the wok, add the soy bean sprouts and bean curd pockets, mix and heat evenly; remove and arrange onto a plate, cool. Season with **2** and serve.

1

2

雪菜百頁
Stir-fried Bean Curd Sheets and Salted Mustards

雪裡紅 ...... 1 5 0 公克
百頁 .... 2 0 張

1
鹽、糖 ..... 各¼ 小匙
味精 .... ⅛ 小匙

2
高湯 .... ½ 杯
麻油、鹽 ... 各½ 小匙
糖、味精 ... 各¼ 小匙

3
水 .... 1 小匙
太白粉 .... ½ 小匙

150g (5¼oz.) salted mustard greens
20 sheets .... bean curd sheet (Pai-Yeh)

1 •¼t. each: salt, sugar

2
•½C. stock
•½t.each: sesame oil, salt
•¼t. sugar

3
•1t. water
•½t. cornstarch

1 將處理過的百頁撕成適當大小，雪裡紅洗淨切末備用。
2 鍋熱入油 2 大匙燒熱，入雪裡紅及 **1** 料炒香後盛起，另鍋熱入油 1 大匙燒熱，入百頁、**2** 料以小火煮約 1 0 分鐘，再入炒過之雪裡紅拌炒均勻，以 **3** 料芶芡即可。

1 Tear the prepared bean curd sheets into bite size pieces. Wash and mince the salted mustard greens.
2 Heat the wok, add 2T. oil and heat. Fry the salted mustard greens and **1** until fragrant, remove. Heat another wok, add 1T. oil and heat. Cook the bean curd sheets and **2** over low heat for 10 minutes. Add the fried salted mustard greens and stir-fry evenly; thicken with **3**, and serve.

雞火干絲
Bean Curd Noodles with Chicken and Ham

白色四方豆干　2 0 0 公克
雞胸肉 .... 1 5 0 公克
中式火腿 .... 7 0 公克

200g(7oz.) ..... white pressed bean curd squares
150g(5¼oz.) . chicken breast
70g(2⅓oz.) ...... Chinese ham

1 雞胸肉、中式火腿洗淨後加 4 杯水蒸約 3 0 分鐘後，取出雞胸肉及中式火腿分別切絲排入湯碗內，肉湯留用。
2 豆乾切細絲入肉湯煮開後，沖入湯碗中即可。

1 Wash the chicken breast and ham, add 4C. water and steam for 30 minutes. Remove from the pot; save the soup. Cut the chicken breast and ham into julienne strips, arrange in a soup bowl.
2 Cut the pressed bean curd into julienne strips, add to the soup and bring to a boil. Pour into the soup bowl, and serve.

蛤蜊 ‥‥‥‥ 3 0 0 公克	300g(10½oz.) ‥‥‥‥‥.clams
蛋 ‥‥‥‥‥‥ 4 個	4 ‥‥‥‥‥‥‥‥‥‥‥‥‥eggs

1
- 高湯 ‥‥‥‥ 1½ 杯
- 薑酒汁 ‥‥‥ 1 大匙
- 鹽 ‥‥‥‥‥ ½ 小匙
- 味精 ‥‥‥‥ ¼ 小匙

1
- •1½C. stock
- •1T. ginger juice wine
- •½t. salt

1 蛤蜊泡水吐沙，洗淨備用。
2 水 2 杯煮開，入蛤蜊用小火煮至蛤蜊殼微開即熄火，將蛤蜊取出置蒸碗內，取湯汁 1 杯待涼備用。
3 蛋打散入 **1** 料及蛤蜊湯汁拌勻，再倒入蒸碗內，入鍋蒸 1 0 分鐘，熄火再燜 5 分鐘即可。
■ 薑酒汁的做法：薑先磨成泥，再濾去薑渣，然後與酒以 1：1 之比例混合均勻即為薑酒汁。

1 Soak the clams to get rid of the sand and wash thoroughly.
2 Bring 2C. water to a boil, add the clams and cook over low heat until the clams open; transfer the clams to a steam bowl. Keep 1C. soup; cool for later use.
3 Beat the eggs, mix well with **1** and the clam soup. Pour the mixture over the clams. Steam for 10 minutes, turn off heat and let sit for 5 minutes covered. Serve.
■ Ginger Juice Wine: Mash ginger, save the juice and discard the remnants. Mix 1 part ginger juice with 1 part cooking wine.

雪裡紅 ‥‥‥‥ 7 0 公克	70g(2½oz.) ..salted mustard greens
蛋 ‥‥‥‥‥‥ 4 個	4 ‥‥‥‥‥‥‥‥‥‥‥‥‥eggs
蔥末 ‥‥‥‥‥ 4 大匙	4T. ‥‥‥minced green onion

1
- 高湯 ‥‥‥‥‥ ½ 杯
- 鹽 ‥‥‥‥‥‥ ½ 小匙
- 糖、味精 ‥‥各¼ 小匙

1
- •½C. stock
- •½t. salt
- •¼t. sugar

2 酒、糖 ‥‥‥各¼ 小匙

2
- •¼t. each: cooking wine, sugar

1 雪裡紅洗淨切末，蛋打散加 **1** 料拌勻備用。
2 鍋熱入油 3 大匙燒熱，入蔥末爆香，續入雪裡紅及 **2** 料拌炒均勻，再入蛋液拌炒至蛋液稍為凝固即可。

1 Wash and mince the salted mustard greens. Beat the eggs and mix well with **1**.
2 Heat the wok, add 3T. oil and heat. Fry the green onions until fragrant. Mix in the salted mustard greens and **2**, stir-fry evenly. Add the beaten eggs and fry until the eggs turn solid. Serve.

炸響鈴
Crispy Ding-Dong Bells

雞胸肉 . . . . 2 5 公克
豆皮 . . . . 4 張

1
蛋黃 . . . . 1/4 個
太白粉 . . . . 3/4 小匙
紹興酒、鹽、味精 . . .
. . . . 各 1/8 小匙

25g(1oz.) . . . . chicken breast
4 sheets bean curd skin

1
- 1/4 egg yoke
- 3/4 t. cornstarch
- 1/8 t. each: Chinese Shao-Shin wine, salt

1

1 雞胸肉剁成泥，入 **1** 料拌勻後分成 4 等份。
2 將豆皮周圍的硬邊裁掉（圖 1），再將一份肉泥塗於豆皮較長之一邊，成為寬 5 公分之帶狀（圖 2），再由沒塗肉泥的一邊捲起成圓筒狀（不宜太緊）（圖 3），依續做成 4 捲後，切成 3 . 5 公分段備用。
3 鍋熱入油 3 杯燒至六分熱（約 1 4 0 ℃），入豆皮捲炸至金黃色（炸時須不斷翻動），撈起瀝乾即可。
■ 響鈴可配甜麵醬加蔥白，或配椒鹽食用。

2

1 Finely chop the chicken into paste; mix in **1** evenly, separate into 4 portions.
2 Remove the hard outer rim of the bean curd skins (Fig. 1). Spread 1 portion of the chicken paste with a width of 5 cm (2") at the longer side of the bean curd skins (Fig. 2) Roll the bean curd skins into a cylinder from the part where there is no meat (do not roll too tight, Fig. 3). After finishing rolling 4 rolls, cut into 3.5 cm (1 1/4") sections.
3 Heat the wok, add 3C. oil and heat to 140°C (280°F). Deep-fry the bean curd skin rolls until golden brown, turning continuously. Remove from oil; serve.
■ Crispy Ding-Dong Bells may be served with sweet soy bean paste and the white part of green onions or Szechwan pepper salt.

3

花蟹（１隻） ５００公克
嫩豆腐 .... 1 1/2 塊
胡蘿蔔末 .... 1/3 杯
雞油 .... ２ 大匙
蔥末、薑末 ...... 各 1 大匙

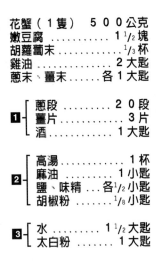

1
蔥段 ２０段
薑片 ３片
酒 .... 1 大匙

2
高湯 .... 1 杯
麻油 .... 1 小匙
鹽、味精 ... 各 1/2 小匙
胡椒粉 .... 1/8 小匙

3
水 .... 1 1/2 大匙
太白粉 .... 1 大匙

1 (500g or 1lb.) .... crab
1 1/2 blocks ...... soft bean curd
1/3 C. .... minced carrot
2T. .... chicken fat
1T. each: minced green onion, minced ginger

1
•20 sections green onion
•3 slices ginger
•1T. cooking wine

2
•1C. stock
•1t. sesame oil
•1/2 t. salt
•1/8 t. pepper

3
•1 1/2 T. water
•1T. cornstarch

1 花蟹洗淨，切下蟹螯以刀背拍碎，蟹身切成４塊，加**1**料大火蒸１０分鐘後，將蟹肉取出備用。
2 豆腐切１.５公分立方小塊，入鍋煮１分鐘後撈起瀝乾備用。
3 鍋熱入雞油２大匙燒熱，入蔥末、薑末爆香後，續入胡蘿蔔、豆腐及**2**料煮開，改小火煮１５分鐘，再入蟹肉煮約１０分鐘，最後以**3**料芶芡即可。

1 Wash the crab, snip off the claws and crack the claws with the back of a knife. Cut the crab into 4 pieces, add **1** ; steam over high heat for 10 minutes, remove the crab meat.
2 Cut the bean curd into 1.5 cm (1/2") cubes; blanch in boiling water; remove and drain.
3 Heat the wok, add 2T. chicken fat and heat. Fry the green onions and the ginger until fragrant. Mix in the carrot, bean curd, and **2**; bring to a boil. Reduce to low heat and simmer for 15 minutes. Add the crab meat and cook for 10 minutes; thicken with **3** , and serve.

冬菇腐衣
Black Mushrooms and Bean Curd Skin

扁尖、熟青豆仁各３０公克
香菇 ２０公克
豆皮 ４張
麻油 １小匙

1
高湯 .... ¹/₂ 杯
糖 .... ¹/₄ 小匙

2
高湯 .... ¹/₂ 杯
醬油 ...... １¹/₂ 大匙
糖 .... ¹/₄ 小匙
味精、胡椒粉各¹/₈ 小匙

30g(1oz.) each: ..... dried
bamboo shoots, boiled
green peas
20g(²/₃oz.) .... dried black
mushrooms
4 sheets .... bean curd
skin
1t. .... sesame oil

1
• ¹/₂C. stock
• ¹/₄t. sugar

2
• ¹/₂C. stock
• 1¹/₂T. soy sauce
• ¹/₄t. sugar
• ¹/₈t. pepper

1 扁尖（圖１）洗淨泡水至軟（約３０分鐘），切２公分斜片（圖２），香菇泡軟去蒂斜切１公分條狀，豆皮泡軟，撕成適當大小備用。
2 鍋熱入油２大匙燒熱，入香菇爆香後，入扁尖拌炒一下，續入 **1** 料以小火煮約１０分鐘，再入豆皮拌炒均勻，最後入 **2** 料煮約５分鐘，起鍋前再灑入青豆仁、麻油即可。

1 Wash the dried bamboo shoots (Fig. 1), soak in the water until soft (about 30 minutes); cut into 2 cm (1") slanted slices (Fig. 2). Soak the mushrooms until soft, discard the stems, cut into 1 cm (¹/₂") slanted slices. Soak the bean curd skin until soft, then tear into serving size pieces.
2 Heat the wok, add 2T. oil and heat. Fry the mushrooms until fragrant, add the bamboo shoots and stir-fry slightly. Stir in **1** and cook over low heat for 10 minutes. Mix in the bean curd skins and stir evenly. Add **2** and cook for 5 minutes; sprinkle on the boiled green peas and the sesame oil, remove. Serve.

1

2

草蝦仁（小）　２２０公克
嫩豆腐 .... 1 1/2 塊
蔥末、雞油 ...... 各 2 大匙

1
太白粉 .... 2 小匙
酒 ....1/2 小匙
鹽 ....1/4 小匙
蛋白 ....1/3 個

2
高湯 .... 1 杯
鹽、麻油 ... 各1/2 小匙
味精 ....1/4 小匙

3
水 .... 1 1/2 大匙
太白粉 .... 1 大匙

220g(8oz.) .... small
fresh water shrimp
1¹/₂ blocks ...... soft bean
curd (tofu)
2T. each: minced green
onion, chicken fat

1
•2t. cornstarch
•1/2t. cooking wine
•1/4t. salt
•1/3 egg white

2
•1C. stock
•1/2t. each: salt,
sesame oil

3
•1¹/₂T. water
•1T. cornstarch

1 蝦仁去腸泥洗淨擦乾水份，入 **1** 料拌勻醃約２０分鐘，嫩豆腐切１公分立方小塊備用。
2 鍋熱入油 3 大匙燒熱，入蝦仁炒熟盛起，另鍋熱入雞油 2 大匙燒熱，入蔥末 1 大匙爆香後，續入
豆腐及 **2** 料小火煮２０分鐘，再入蝦仁拌勻，並以 **3** 料苟芡，最後灑上剩餘蔥末即可。

1 Shell and devein the shrimp with toothpicks, pat dry; marinate in **1** for 20 minutes. Cut the
bean curd into 1 cm (¹/₂") cubes.
2 Heat the wok, add 3T. oil and heat. Fry the shrimp until cooked, remove. Heat another wok,
add 2T. chicken fat and heat. Stir-fry 1T. minced green onion until fragrant; mix in the bean
curd and **2**, cook over low heat for 20 minutes. Add the shrimp and mix well, thicken with
3; sprinkle with the remaining minced green onion, and serve.

素黃雀
Vegetarian Sparrow Rolls

青江菜	8 0 公克	80g(2³/₄oz.)	bok choy
豆干	5 0 公克	50g(1³/₄oz.)	pressed bean curds
扁尖	2 0 公克	20g(²/₃oz.)	dried bamboo shoots
香菇	1 0 公克	10g(¹/₃oz.)	dried black mushrooms
豆皮	4 張	4 sheets	bean curd skin

1
糖、麻油 .... 各 1 小匙
鹽、味精、胡椒粉 各 ¹/₈ 小匙

1
•1t. each: sugar, sesame oil
•¹/₈t. each: salt, pepper

2
水 .... 1 杯
醬油 .... 1 ¹/₂ 小匙
糖 .... 1 小匙
味精 .... ¹/₃ 小匙

2
•1C. water
•1¹/₂t. soy sauce
•1t. sugar

3
水 .... 1 小匙
太白粉 .... ¹/₂ 小匙

3
•1t. water
•¹/₂t. cornstarch

1 香菇泡軟去蒂切末，扁尖泡水半小時瀝乾切末，豆干、青江菜洗淨亦切末，入 **1** 料拌勻即為內餡，分成 8 等份備用。
2 豆皮 4 張對切成 8 張（圖 1），每張豆皮包 1 份內餡，捲起成長條狀（圖 2），再打結即為黃雀（圖 3）。
3 鍋熱入油 6 杯燒至七分熱（ 1 6 0 ℃），入黃雀炸成金黃色撈起瀝油備用。
4 **2** 料煮開，入炸好的黃雀一起燜煮 5 分鐘，再入 **3** 料勾芡即可。

1 Soak the mushrooms until soft, discard the stems, and mince. Soak the dried bamboo shoots in water for 30 minutes, then drain and mince. Wash and mince the pressed bean curds and bok choy; mix **1** with the ingredients thoroughly. Divide into 8 portions.
2 Cut four sheets of the bean curd skin into halves to make 8 equal sheets (Fig. 1). To make the "vegetarian sparrows," (Fig. 3) wrap one portion of the filling in the bean curd skin, roll up lengthwise (Fig. 2), and tie a knot.
3 Heat the wok, add 6C. oil and heat to 160°C (320°F). Deep-fry the "vegetarian sparrows" until golden brown, remove from oil and drain.
4 Bring **2** to a boil, add the "vegetarian sparrows," and simmer for 5 minutes; thicken with **3**, and serve.

1   2   3

炒雙冬
Stir-fried Bamboo Shoots and Mushrooms

筍（淨重）... ３００公克
小豆苗（圖１）１５０公克
香菇...........２０公克
蔥段 .... ８ 段
麻油 .... １ 小匙

1
水..............¹/₄ 杯
醬油 ...... １ ¹/₂ 小匙
糖 ....¹/₂ 小匙
鹽 ....¹/₄ 小匙

2
水 .... １ 小匙
太白粉 ......¹/₂ 小匙

300g(10¹/₂oz.,net weight)
............bamboo shoots
150g(5¹/₃oz.) .....pea pod
tips (Fig. 1)
20g(²/₃oz.) ....dried black
mushrooms
8 sections ..green onion
1t. ....sesame oil

1
- ¹/₄C. water
- 1¹/₂t. soy sauce
- ¹/₂t. sugar
- ¹/₄t. salt

2
- 1t. water
- ¹/₂t. cornstarch

1 筍洗淨切滾刀塊（圖２），香菇泡軟去蒂洗淨，小豆苗洗淨均備用。
2 鍋熱入油 2 杯燒至三分熱（８０℃），入筍炸 5 分鐘，取出瀝油備用。
3 鍋內留油 2 大匙燒熱，入小豆苗炒熟，盛起排入盤中。
4 鍋熱入油 3 大匙燒熱，入蔥段爆香，續入筍及**1**料，以中火煮 7 分鐘，再入香菇煮 3 分鐘，以**2**料芶芡並淋上麻油，起鍋排於豆苗上即可。

1 Wash the bamboo shoots, then roll-cut (Fig. 2). Soak the mushrooms until soft, discard the stems, then wash. Wash the pea pod tips.
2 Heat the wok, add 2T. oil and heat to 80°C (180°F). Deep-fry the bamboo shoots for 5 minutes, remove from the oil and drain.
3 Keep 2T. oil, and reheat. Fry the pea pod tips until cooked; remove and arrange on a plate.
4 Heat the wok, add 3T. oil and heat. Fry the green onions until fragrant; mix in the bamboo shoots and **1**, cook over medium heat for about 7 minutes. Add the mushrooms and cook for 3 minutes. Thicken with **2**, and sprinkle on the sesame oil. Remove, arrange the bamboo shoots and mushrooms on top of the pea pod tips, and serve.

1

2

Emerald Mushrooms

草菇、洋菇　各２００公克
芥藍菜（圖1）１５０公克
蔥末 １大匙
麻油、鹽 各１小匙

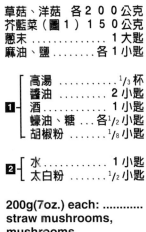

1
┌ 高湯 ....¹/₃ 杯
│ 醬油 ２小匙
│ 酒............ １小匙
│ 蠔油、糖 ...各¹/₂ 小匙
└ 胡椒粉 ....¹/₈ 小匙

2
┌ 水 １小匙
└ 太白粉 ....¹/₂ 小匙

200g(7oz.) each: ....
straw mushrooms,
mushrooms
150g(5¹/₄oz.) .... gailan
(Fig. 1)
1T..minced green onion
1t. each:sesame oil, salt

1
- •¹/₃C. stock
- •2t. soy sauce
- •1t. cooking wine
- •¹/₂t. each: oyster sauce, sugar
- •¹/₈t. pepper

2
- •1t. water
- •¹/₂t. cornstarch

1 水４杯煮開，入洗淨之草菇、洋菇及鹽煮５分鐘，起鍋後入冷水漂涼再瀝乾水份。芥藍菜洗淨備用。
2 水５杯煮開，入油１大匙及芥藍菜煮熟，取出瀝乾水份並攤開放涼，再排盤備用。
3 鍋熱入油３大匙燒熱，入蔥末爆香，續入洋菇、草菇及**1**料炒拌均勻後，以中火燒煮１０分鐘，再以**2**料芶茨並淋上麻油，起鍋置於芥藍菜上即可。

1 Bring 4C. water to a boil; add the washed straw mushrooms, mushrooms and salt, cook for 5 minutes. Remove, rinse under cold water, and drain. Wash the gailan.
2 Bring 5C. water to a boil. Add 1T. oil and the gailan to boiling water and cook until done; remove, drain, and spread out to cool. Arrange on a plate.
3 Heat the wok, add 3T. oil and heat. Fry the green onion until fragrant, mix in the straw mushrooms, mushrooms, and **1**; stir-fry evenly. Cook over medium heat for 10 minutes, thicken with **2**, sprinkle on the sesame oil. Pour mixture over the gailan. Serve.

1

鹹菜豆板酥
Mashed Beans with Salted Mustard Greens

蠶豆仁	300公克	300g (10½oz.) .. broad beans
黃色雪裡紅	70公克	70g (2½oz.) ..... yellow salted mustard greens
高湯	1¾ 杯	1¾C. .... stock
糖	1 小匙	1t. .... sugar

1 雪裡紅洗淨泡水10分鐘後，瀝乾水份並切細丁，蠶豆仁洗淨備用。
2 鍋熱入油3杯燒至七分熱（160℃），入雪裡紅炸至金黃色，取出瀝油備用。
3 鍋內留油5大匙燒熱，入蠶豆仁拌炒數下，再入高湯1½杯以中火煮10分鐘後，以鍋鏟將蠶豆壓成泥，再加高湯¼杯拌勻，最後再入雪裡紅及糖拌炒均勻即可。

1 Wash the salted mustard greens, soak in the water for 10 minutes, drain and mince. Wash the beans.
2 Heat the wok, add 3C. oil and heat to 160°C (320°F). Deep-fry the salted mustard greens until golden brown, remove and drain.
3 Keep 5T. oil and reheat. Stir-fry the beans several times, add 1½C. stock, and cook over medium heat for 10 minutes. Mash the beans with a spatula, add ¼C. stock, and mix thoroughly. Stir in the salted mustard greens and sugar, fry evenly, and serve.

竹笙絲瓜
Sing Qua with Dried Bamboo Piths

澎湖絲瓜	600公克	600g(1⅓lbs.) . angled loofah (sing qua)
竹笙	10公克	10g(⅓oz.) ...... dried bamboo piths (shu sheng)
高湯	1杯	1C. .... stock
麻油	1小匙	1t. .... sesame oil

1	高湯	1 杯	**1**	•1C. stock
	鹽	1 小匙		•1t. salt
	糖	½ 小匙		•½t. sugar
	胡椒粉	⅛ 小匙		•⅛t. pepper

2	水	1 小匙	**2**	•1t. water
	太白粉	½ 小匙		•½t. cornstarch

1 竹笙泡水30分鐘後洗淨，瀝乾水份，切4公分長段，絲瓜去皮洗淨切4公分長條備用。
2 高湯1杯入竹笙煮5分鐘，撈出瀝乾水份。
3 鍋熱入油3大匙燒熱，入絲瓜拌炒片刻，續入■料將絲瓜煮熟，再入竹笙煮3分鐘，最後以■料芶芡並淋上麻油即可。

1 Soak the bamboo piths in water for 30 minutes, wash and drain. Cut the bamboo piths into 4 cm (1½") long sections. Pare the angled loofah, wash, cut into 4 cm (1½") long pieces.
2 Add 1C. stock to the bamboo piths, cook for 5 minutes; remove and drain.
3 Heat the wok, add 3T. oil and heat. Stir-fry the angled loofah quickly; add **1** and fry until cooked. Stir in the bamboo piths and cook for 3 minutes, thicken with **2**; sprinkle on the sesame oil. Serve.

蔥爆蠶豆

Stir-fried Broad Beans with Green Onions

蠶豆仁 ３５０公克	350g(12¹/₃oz.) ... broad beans
雞油 ３大匙	3T. .... chicken fat
蔥末 ２大匙	2T. .... minced green onion

1 ⎡ 高湯 .... 1¹/₂ 杯   **1** • 1¹/₂C. stock
   ⎣ 鹽 .... ¹/₂ 小匙   • ¹/₂t. salt

1 蠶豆仁洗淨瀝乾水份備用。
2 鍋熱入油４杯燒至三分熱（８０℃），入蠶豆仁炸熟，取出瀝油。
3 另鍋熱入雞油燒熱，入蔥末爆香，再入蠶豆仁及**1**料拌炒均勻，以中火煮１０分鐘即可。

1 Wash the broad beans, drain.
2 Heat the wok, add 4C. oil and heat to 80℃ (180˚F). Deep-fry the broad beans until cooked, remove from the oil and drain.
3 Heat another wok, add the chicken fat and heat. Fry the green onions until fragrant. Mix in the broad beans and **1**, stir-fry evenly. Cook over medium heat for 10 minutes and serve.

火腿蠶豆筍

Broad Beans with Ham and Bamboo Shoots

蠶豆仁 ２５０公克	250g(8³/₄oz.) ..... broad beans
筍（淨重）... １００公克	100g(3¹/₂oz., net weight) ...... bamboo shoots
中式火腿 ２０公克	20g(²/₃oz.) .... Chinese ham
麻油 １小匙	1t. .... sesame oil

1 ⎡ 高湯 .... 1¹/₂ 杯   **1** • 1¹/₂C. stock
   ⎢ 酒 .... ¹/₂ 小匙   • ¹/₂t. cooking wine
   ⎣ 鹽 .... ¹/₄ 小匙   • ¹/₄t. salt

2 ⎡ 水 .... １小匙   **2** • 1t. water
   ⎣ 太白粉 ...... ¹/₂ 小匙   • ¹/₂t. cornstarch

1 蠶豆仁洗淨瀝乾水份，筍及火腿均洗淨切小丁備用。
2 鍋熱入油３大匙燒熱，入蠶豆仁及筍拌炒，續入**1**料煮開，改中火煮１０分鐘後，再入火腿丁拌炒均勻，最後以**2**料勾芡並淋上麻油即可。

1 Wash the beans, drain. Wash the bamboo shoots and ham; cut both into small cubes.
2 Heat the wok, add 3T. oil and heat. Stir-fry the beans and the bamboo shoots, add **1** and bring to a boil. Reduce to medium heat and cook for 10 minutes. Add the ham and stir thoroughly; thicken with **2**, sprinkle with the sesame oil. Serve.

雪菜春筍
Spring Bamboo Shoots and Salted Mustards

| 筍（淨重）... ３００公克 | 300g(10½oz., net weight) .... bamboo shoots |
| 雪裡紅...... １５０公克 | 150g(5¼oz.) .... salted mustard greens |

1 ┌ 水 .... ¼ 杯
　　├ 糖 .... 1 小匙
　　└ 鹽 .... ½ 小匙

1 ┌ •¼C. water
　　├ •1t. sugar
　　└ •½t. salt

1 筍洗淨切薄片。雪裡紅洗淨泡水１０分鐘後切末。
2 鍋熱入油３大匙燒熱，入雪裡紅炒香，取出備用。另鍋熱入油３大匙燒熱，入筍片炒片刻，再入**1**料並蓋上鍋蓋燜煮３分鐘後，入雪裡紅拌勻即可。

1 Wash the bamboo shoots, cut into thin slices. Wash the salted mustard greens, soak in water for 10 minutes; drain and mince.
2 Heat the wok, add 3T. oil and heat. Fry the salted mustard greens until fragrant, remove. Heat the wok, add 3T. oil and heat. Fry the bamboo shoots quickly, stir in **1**, cover the wok and simmer for 3 minutes. Add the salted mustard greens, mix well. Serve.

雞油豌豆
Baby Snow Peas in Chicken Broth

豌豆仁....... １２０公克	120g(4⅓oz.) .... baby snow peas
中式火腿....... ２０公克	20g(⅔oz.) .... Chinese ham
雞油 .... ½ 小匙	½t. .... chicken fat

1 ┌ 高湯 .... 2 杯
　　└ 鹽 .... ½ 小匙

1 ┌ •2C. stock
　　└ •½t. salt

2 ┌ 水 .... 1 大匙
　　└ 太白粉 .... 1 小匙

2 ┌ •1T. water
　　└ •1t. cornstarch

1 豌豆仁洗淨瀝乾水份，中式火腿洗淨蒸熟切末備用。
2 **1**料煮開，入豌豆仁煮１分鐘，再入**2**料芶芡，並淋上雞油拌勻，起鍋灑上火腿末即可。

1 Wash the peas, drain. Wash and steam the ham until cooked, then mince.
2 Bring **1** to a boil, add the peas and cook for 1 minute; thicken with **2**. Sprinkle this mixture with chicken fat, mix well. Remove from the pot, sprinkle on the ham, and serve.

干貝毛豆仁
Fresh Soy Beans and Dried Scallops

毛豆仁 200公克	200g(7oz.) ..fresh soy beans
干貝 30公克	30g(1oz.) .... dried scallops
酒 1小匙	1t. .... cooking wine

1
- 麻油 2小匙
- 鹽 1/2小匙
- 味精、胡椒粉各1/8小匙

1
- •2t. sesame oil
- •1/2t. salt
- •1/8t. pepper

1 干貝加水3/4杯及酒，入鍋蒸1小時，取出瀝乾水份，剝絲備用。
2 水5杯煮開，入毛豆仁煮10分鐘，取出入冷水中漂涼後，將外皮剝掉，再入開水中煮開，隨即取出瀝乾水份，入**1**料與干貝絲拌勻即可。

1 Add 3/4C. water and 1t. cooking wine to the scallops; steam for 1 hour, remove and drain. Tear the scallops into fine shreds.
2 Bring 5C. water to a boil, add the soy beans and cook for 10 minutes. Remove from heat and rinse under cold water. Peel the skin from beans. Put the soy beans in the boiling water, bring to a boil; remove and drain. Mix **1** and the scallops thoroughly and serve.

醬蘿蔔
Marinated Turnips

白蘿蔔（淨重）500公克	500g(1lb., net weight) .... turnips

1
- 鹽 1大匙
- 花椒粒 1小匙
- 八角 2顆

1
- •1T. salt
- •1t. Szechwan peppercorns
- •2 pieces star anise

2
- 糖 2 1/2大匙
- 醬油 2大匙

2
- •2 1/2T. sugar
- •2T. soy sauce

1 白蘿蔔去皮洗淨切成四瓣，再切薄片，入**1**料拌勻，用重物壓2小時，取出瀝乾水份，用布包好再用重物壓1小時，再入**2**料拌勻，醃1小時即可。
■ 若未立即食用，冷藏可保存2天。

1 Pare and wash the turnips, cut each into 4 equal pieces; slice thin. Mix **1** with the turnips well. Place a heavy weight on the turnips for 2 hours; remove the weight and drain off the excess liquid. Wrap the turnips in a cloth, press again with a heavy weight for 1 hour, mix with **2** thoroughly, and marinate for 1 hour. Serve.
■ If not served immediately, may be kept in a refrigerator up to 2 days.

如意菜
Vegetarian Good Luck

黄豆芽 300公克	300g(10½oz.) ....soy bean sprouts
小白菜 200公克	200g(7oz.) .....baby cabbage
鹽 .... ½小匙	½t. ....salt

1 糖、鹽 .... 各½小匙　　**1** •½t. each: sugar, salt

1 黄豆芽洗淨瀝乾水份，小白菜洗淨切段。
2 鍋熱入油 3 大匙燒熱，入黄豆芽及**1**料炒熟，取出備用。
3 另鍋熱入油 3 大匙燒熱，入小白菜及鹽炒熟，再入黄豆芽拌勻即可。

1 Wash and drain the soy bean sprouts; wash the baby cabbage and cut into sections.
2 Heat the wok, add 3T. oil and heat. Fry the soy bean sprouts and **1** until cooked, remove.
3 Heat the wok, add 3T. oil and heat. Fry the baby cabbage and season with the salt until cooked. Mix in the soy bean sprouts evenly, and serve.

油燜筍
Braised Bamboo Shoots

| 桂竹筍 .... 450公克 | 450g(1lb.) ....boiled bamboo shoots |
| **1** 醬油 .... 2 大匙　糖 .... 1 大匙　鹽 .... ¾小匙 | **1** •2T. soy sauce •1T. sugar •¾t. salt |

1 桂竹筍洗淨，剝絲後切 4 公分長段，水 10 杯煮開，入桂竹筍絲煮 50 分鐘，撈起入冷水漂涼，瀝乾水份備用。
2 鍋熱入油½杯燒熱，入筍絲及**1**料拌炒，再入水 1½ 杯煮開，蓋上鍋蓋以小火續煮 20 分鐘，至湯汁收乾，再入水 1½ 杯小火煮 20 分鐘至湯汁收乾即可。

1 Wash the bamboo shoots, shred and cut into 4 cm (1½") long sections. Cook the bamboo shoots in 10C. boiling water for 50 minutes; remove from pot, rinse under cold water, and drain.
2 Heat the wok, add ½C. oil and heat. Stir-fry the bamboo shoots and **1**, add 1½C. water and bring to a boil. Cover, cook over low heat until the water has evaporated (about 20 minutes). Add 1½C. water and simmer for 20 minutes until the water has evaporated. Serve.

油燜涼瓜
Braised Bitter Melon

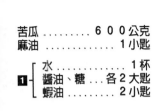

苦瓜 600公克	600g(1¹/₃lbs.) .... bitter melon
麻油 1小匙	1t. .... sesame oil

1
水 1杯
醬油、糖 ... 各2大匙
蝦油 2小匙

1
- 1C. water
- 2T. each: soy sauce, sugar
- 2t. shrimp oil

1 苦瓜洗淨切對半去籽,用湯匙將內層薄膜刨乾淨,洗淨切大塊。
2 水6杯煮開,入苦瓜煮10分鐘,取出入冷水漂涼,瀝乾備用。
3 鍋熱入油6大匙燒熱,入苦瓜炒熟,入**1**料調味,以中火煮至湯汁收乾(約30分鐘),最後入麻油拌勻即可。

1 Wash and halve the bitter melon, discard the seeds. Scoop out the inner membrane of the bitter melon with a spoon; wash and cut into large pieces.
2 Cook the bitter melon in 6C. boiling water for 10 minutes; remove and rinse under cold water, drain.
3 Heat the wok, add 6T. oil and heat. Fry the bitter melon until cooked, season with **1**. Cook over medium heat until sauce has evaporated (about 30 minutes). Mix well with the sesame oil and serve.

奶油菜膽
Vegetables in Cream Sauce

白菜心 300公克	300g(10¹/₂oz.) .... small Chinese cabbage hearts
中式火腿 20公克	20g(²/₃oz.) .... Chinese ham
麵粉 2大匙	2T. .... flour

1
水 1杯
奶水 3大匙
鹽、雞油 ... 各1小匙

1
- 1C. water
- 3T. evaporated milk
- 1t. each: salt, chicken fat

1 白菜心洗淨瀝乾水份,中式火腿洗淨蒸熟切末備用。
2 鍋熱入油3大匙燒熱,入白菜心拌炒數下,再入水 ¹/₂ 杯煮10分鐘,取出排入盤中。
3 另鍋熱入油3大匙燒熱,入麵粉小火炒香,再入**1**料拌勻煮開,淋在白菜心上並灑上火腿末即可。
■ 白菜心可以青江菜或白菜取代。

1 Wash and drain the small Chinese cabbage. Wash and steam the ham until cooked; mince.
2 Heat the wok, add 3T. oil and heat. Stir-fry the small Chinese cabbage hearts several times, add ¹/₂C. water, and cook for 10 minutes. Remove and arrange on a plate.
3 Heat another wok, add 3T. oil and heat. Fry the flour over low heat until fragrant; add **1** and mix well; bring to a boil. Pour mixture over the cabbage, then sprinkle the ham on the cabbage. Serve.
■ Small Chinese cabbage hearts may be substituted with bok choy or cabbage.

宋嫂魚羹
Madam Sung's Fish Soup

魚肉（淨肉）	……… 2 3 0 公克		230g(8oz., net weight)	………fish
熟青豆仁	………… 1 5 0 公克		150g(5¼oz.)	….boiled green peas
高湯	……………… 6 杯		6C.	………………………stock
香菜末	………………… ½ 杯		½C.	……………minced coriander

1
- 熟筍丁 ……… 1 0 0 公克
- 中式火腿 ……… 7 5 公克
- 香菇 ……… 1 2 公克

1
- •100g(3½oz.) boiled bamboo shoots
- •75g(2⅔oz.) Chinese ham
- •12g(½oz.) dried black mushrooms

2
- 蔥末 ………… 2 大匙
- 薑末 ………… 2 小匙

2
- •2T. minced green onion
- •2t. minced ginger

3
- 蛋白 ………… 1 個
- 鹽 ………… ½ 小匙

3
- •1 egg white
- •½t. salt

4
- 鹽、糖 ……… 各½ 小匙
- 味精、胡椒粉 …… 各¼ 小匙

4
- •½t. each: salt, sugar
- •¼t. pepper

5
- 水 ………… 4 大匙
- 太白粉 ………… 2 大匙

5
- •4T. water
- •2T. cornstarch

1 魚肉切約 0.6 公分之立方塊，入 **3** 料拌醃，中式火腿洗淨蒸熟後，剝成細絲（圖1），香菇泡軟去蒂切小丁。
2 鍋熱入油½杯燒至五分熱（120℃），入魚肉炒至肉色變白即撈起（圖2），瀝乾備用。
3 鍋中留油 2 大匙燒熱，入 **2** 料爆香，續入 **1** 料炒香，再入高湯煮開後，依次入魚肉、青豆仁及 **4** 料煮開，並以 **5** 料芶芡，熄火起鍋，灑入香菜末即可。
■ 魚肉可選用鯉魚、鱸魚….等。

1 Cut the fish into 0.6 cm. (¼") cubes, marinate in **3**. Wash the ham, steam until done, tear into julienne strips (Fig. 1). Soak the mushrooms until soft, discard the stems, cut into small cubes.
2 Heat the wok, add ½C. oil and heat to 120°C (250°F). Fry the fish until pale, remove from oil (Fig. 2) and drain.
3 Keep 2T. oil in the wok and heat. Fry **2** until fragrant, stir in **1** and fry until pungent. Add the stock and bring to a boil. Mix in the fish, green peas, and **4**; bring to a boil. Thicken with **5**, turn off heat and place in a serving bowl. Sprinkle on the coriander and serve.

1

2

蘿蔔絲鯽魚湯
Gold Carps and Shredded Turnip Soup

鯽魚	3 3 0 公克	330g(11½oz.) ....gold carp
白蘿蔔絲	2 0 0 公克	200g(7oz.) ..shredded turnip
薑絲	2 0 公克	20g(⅔oz.) ..shredded ginger
麻油	½ 小匙	½t. .... sesame oil

1
- 蔥 .... 3 枝
- 薑片 .... 2 片
- 酒 .... 1 大匙

1
- •3 stalks green onion
- •2 slices ginger
- •1T. cooking wine

2
- 鹽 .... 1 ½ 小匙
- 味精 .... ¼ 小匙

2
- •1½t. salt

1 鯽魚洗淨，入開水中煮開隨即撈起漂涼，蔥切 6 公分長段備用。
2 水 6 杯煮開，入蘿蔔絲、鯽魚及 **1** 料煮開，改小火續煮 2 0 分鐘，使蘿蔔絲軟化後，取出蔥、薑，再入 **2** 料調味，隨即熄火起鍋倒入湯碗內，灑上薑絲、麻油即可。

1 Wash the fish; blanch slightly in boiling water; remove; then rinse under cold water. Cut the green onions into 6 cm (2½") sections.
2 Bring 6C. water to a boil; add the turnips, fish and **1**; bring to a boil. Reduce to low heat and simmer for 20 minutes, until the turnips are soft. Discard the green onions and the ginger; season with **2**. Turn off heat immediately, place in a soup bowl. Sprinkle with ginger and sesame oil. Serve.

蘿蔔絲蛤蜊湯
Clams and Shredded Turnip Soup

蛤蜊	6 0 0 公克	600g(1⅓lbs.) .... clams
白蘿蔔	2 0 0 公克	200g(7oz.) .... turnips
薑	3 0 公克	30g(1oz.) .... ginger

1
- 酒 .... 1 大匙
- 鹽 .... 1 ¼ 小匙
- 味精、麻油 各¼ 小匙

1
- •1T. cooking wine
- •1¼t. salt
- •¼t. sesame oil

1 蛤蜊泡水吐沙洗淨，蘿蔔及薑洗淨後均去皮切絲備用。
2 水 6 杯煮開，入蘿蔔絲煮開後，蓋鍋蓋改小火煮 1 5 分鐘至蘿蔔絲軟化，再入蛤蜊、薑絲及 **1** 料煮至蛤蜊殼張開即可。

1 Soak the clams in water to remove sand, wash. Wash and pare the skin of the turnips and ginger; cut both to julienne strips.
2 Bring 6C. water to a boil in a pot, add the turnips and bring to a boil again. Cover the pot, reduce to low heat and simmer for 15 minutes until the turnips are soft. Mix in the clams, ginger and **1**; cook until the clams open. Serve.

黃豆肉絲湯
Shredded Pork and Soy Beans Soup

豬大骨 .... 4 0 0 公克	400g(14oz.) .... pork bones
黃豆 .... 2 0 0 公克	200g(7oz.) .... soy beans
里肌肉 ...... 1 0 0 公克	100g(3½oz.) .... pork fillet

1 ┌ 鹽 .... 1 小匙
   └ 味精 .... ⅛ 小匙

1 •1t. salt

1 黃豆洗淨，泡水冷藏 2 4 小時，大骨亦洗淨，入開水中煮片刻後，撈起洗淨，里肌肉切絲備用。
2 水 1 2 杯入黃豆及大骨煮開，蓋鍋蓋改小火燜煮 3 小時後，取出大骨，入肉絲再煮開，並以**1**料調味即可。

1 Wash and soak the soy beans, cool in the refrigerator for 24 hours. Wash the pork bones, blanch in boiling water; remove and wash again. Cut the pork fillet into julienne strips.
2 Bring 12C. water, the soy beans, and pork bones to a boil. Cover, reduce to low heat, and simmer for 3 hours. Remove the pork bones, stir in the pork strips, and bring to another boil. Season with **1** and serve

火腿扁尖雞
Ham and Chicken Soup

雞（1 隻） 1 4 0 0 公克	1400g(3lbs.) .... chicken
中式火腿 ..... 4 0 0 公克	400g(14oz.) ..... Chinese ham
扁尖 .... 9 0 公克	90g(3⅕oz.) .... dried bamboo shoots

1 ┌ 蔥 .... 3 枝
   └ 酒 .... 1 大匙

1 ┌ •3 stalks green onion
   └ •1T. cooking wine

1 中式火腿洗淨蒸熟，扁尖洗去表皮鹽份，泡水 3 0 分鐘後瀝乾備用，雞洗淨入開水中煮開，隨即取出洗淨備用。
2 水 1 2 杯煮開，入雞、扁尖及**1**料煮開，蓋上鍋蓋改小火煮 1 ½ 小時後，再入火腿煮 4 0 分鐘即可。
■ 吃時將火腿取出切厚片，置於小碟供食。

1 Wash the ham, steam until done. Wash and rinse off the salt from dried bamboo shoots; soak in water for ½ hour, then drain. Wash the chicken and blanch in boiling water; remove and wash again.
2 Bring 12C. water to a boil. Add the chicken, bamboo shoots, and **1**; bring to a boil. Cover, reduce to low heat and simmer for 1½ hours. Add the ham and cook for 40 minutes.
■ Lift out the ham and cut into thick slices. Place the ham slices on a small plate, accompanied by the soup. Serve.

雪菜黃魚湯
Fish with Salted Mustard Green Soup

黃魚（圖1）　４５０公克
黃色雪裡紅 ... １００公克
熟筍 ７０公克
高湯 ６杯

1 蔥末 .... 1 大匙
　 薑末 .... 1/2 小匙

2 紹興酒 .... 1 小匙
　 鹽 .... 1/2 小匙
　 胡椒粉 .... 1/4 小匙
　 味精 .... 1/8 小匙

450g(1lb.) ..... yellow fish
(Fig. 1)
100g(3¹/₂oz.) .... yellow
salted mustard greens
70g(2¹/₂oz.) ...... boiled or
canned bamboo shoots
6C. .... stock

1 •1T. minced green
onion
•¹/₂t. minced ginger

2 •1t. Chinese Shao-
Shin wine
•¹/₂t. salt
•¹/₄t. pepper

1 黃魚洗淨，雪裡紅洗淨切末（圖2），熟筍切細絲備用。
2 鍋熱入油２大匙燒熱，入 **1** 料爆香，續入雪裡紅、筍絲炒香，再入高湯煮開後，入黃魚煮熟並加 **2** 料調味即可。

1 Wash the fish. Wash and mince the salted mustard greens (Fig. 2). Cut the bamboo shoots into julienne strips.
2 Heat the wok, add 2T. oil and heat. Stir-fry **1** until fragrant, stir in the salted mustard greens and bamboo shoots; fry until pungent. Add the stock and bring to a boil; add the fish and cook until the fish is done. Season with **2**, and serve.

1

2

蒓菜（圖1） 　　２２０公克
雞胸肉 １００公克
中式火腿 ６０公克
高湯 ５杯

1 ⎰ 鹽 １小匙
⎱ 糖 1/2小匙
⎱ 味精 1/4小匙

2 ⎰ 水 ４大匙
⎱ 太白粉 ２大匙

220g(8oz.) ..... canned or
bottled water-shield
(Chwun Tsai, Fig. 1)
100g(3 1/2oz.) ...... chicken
breast
60g(2oz.) .... Chinese
ham
5C. .... stock

1 ⎰ •1t. salt
⎱ •1/2t. sugar

2 ⎰ •4T. water
⎱ •2T. cornstarch

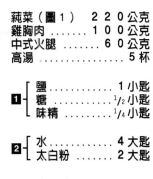

1 雞胸肉洗淨切細絲，加少許水拌勻後，入開水中煮至肉轉白，隨即撈起。中式火腿洗淨切細絲，蒓菜開罐後，用溫水泡洗４至５次，以去除部份酸味，再瀝乾水份備用。
2 高湯煮開，入火腿絲及 **1** 料再煮開，續入 **2** 料芶芡，再入雞絲及蒓菜煮開即可。

1 Wash the chicken breast, cut into julienne strips, add a little water, mix well. Cook chicken in boiling water until white; remove immediately. Wash the Chinese ham and cut into julienne strips. Remove water-shield from the can or bottle, soak and rinse in lukewarm water 4 to 5 times to reduce sour taste; remove and drain.
2 Bring the stock to a boil, mix in the ham and **1**; bring to a boil. Thicken with **2**, stir in the chicken and water-shield; bring to a boil, and serve.

1

醃多鮮
Pork and Salted Pork Soup

五花肉、中式火腿 ....
........各２００公克
冬筍（淨重）　１５０公克
青蒜絲 １０公克
百頁 １０張

200g(7oz.) each: pork belly, Chinese ham
150g(5¼oz., net weight) .... bamboo shoots
10g(⅓oz.) .... shredded garlic leek
10 sheets ...... bean curd sheet

1 已處理過的百頁對切捲成長條（圖１）並打結（圖２），中式火腿洗淨蒸熟，切１.５×０.８公分寬之條狀，五花肉亦切厚片並入水中煮開，隨即撈起，筍切厚片，備用。
3 砂鍋入水１２杯煮開，入五花肉及筍片煮１小時，續入中式火腿煮２０分鐘，再入百頁結煮５分鐘，熄火，灑入青蒜絲即可。

1 Cut the prepared bean curd in half lengthwise (Fig. 1), tie into knots (Fig. 2). Wash the Chinese ham, steam until done; cut into 1.5 cm x 0.8 cm (½"x⅓") strips. Cut the pork belly into thick strips, scald briefly in boiling water, remove. Cut the bamboo shoots into thick slices.
2 Bring 12C. water to a boil in the ceramic pot. Mix in the pork and bamboo shoots, cook for 1 hour. Add the Chinese ham and cook for 20 minutes. Add the bean curd sheets and cook for 5 minutes. Turn off heat, and sprinkle with shredded garlic leek. Serve.

1

2

莧菜黃魚羹

Amaranth and Yellow Fish Pottage

黃魚 ４５０公克
莧菜 ２００公克
高湯 ５杯
紹興酒 １小匙

1〔 豆腐丁 ... １２０公克
　　 熟筍丁 ... １００公克

2〔 水 ４大匙
　　 太白粉 ２大匙

3〔 鹽 １¼小匙
　　 糖 １小匙
　　 胡椒粉 ......¼小匙

450g(1lb.) ..... yellow fish
200g(7oz.) ...... amaranth
5C. .... stock
1t. ... Chinese Shao-Shin wine

1〔 •120g(4¹/₃oz.) diced bean curd
　　 •100g(3¹/₂oz.) diced boiled bamboo shoots

2〔 •4T. water
　　 •2T. cornstarch

3〔 •1¹/₄t. salt
　　 •1t. sugar
　　 •¹/₄t. pepper

1 黃魚洗淨，置於盤上入鍋蒸熟，待涼，用湯匙取肉（圖１），蒸汁留用。
2 莧菜去老纖維（圖２）洗淨，入滾水中煮至軟隨即撈起漂涼，再擠乾水份，剁細備用。
3 鍋入高湯及魚蒸汁煮開，入 **1** 料及魚肉煮開後，以 **2** 料芶芡，再入 **3** 料及莧菜末煮開，起鍋前淋下紹興酒拌勻即可。
■ 雪菜黃魚羹、酸菜黃魚羹：將莧菜黃魚羹之莧菜，以雪裡紅或酸菜葉各１２０公克取代，洗淨後，直接切末烹調，其餘材料及作法與莧菜黃魚羹相同。

1

2

1 Wash the fish, place on a plate and steam the fish until cooked. Cool, then scrape off the fish meat with a spoon (Fig. 1). Keep the fish juice for later use.
2 Wash and discard the tough fibers of amaranth (Fig. 2). Cook in boiling water until soft; remove and rinse under cold water. Squeeze out the water and chop fine.
3 Bring the stock and fish juice to a boil in a wok, mix in **1** and the fish meat; bring to a boil and thicken with **2**. Add **3** and minced amaranth; bring to a boil. Sprinkle with the Chinese Shao-Shin wine, mix well, and serve.
■ Salted Mustard Greens and Yellow Fish Pottage, Sour Mustard and Yellow Fish Pottage: Amaranth may be substituted with 120g(4¹/₃oz.) salted mustard greens or sour mustard. Wash the salted mustard greens or sour mustard, mince and cook directly in fish pottage. The rest of the ingredients and cooking methods are the same as above.

餛飩鴨
Wonton Duck

鴨（1隻）　１６００公克
絞肉 １５０公克
餛飩皮 １００公克
青江菜 6棵
鹽 .... ¹/₂小匙

1
蔥末 1大匙
麻油 .... ³/₄小匙
醬油、糖、酒各¹/₂小匙
鹽 .... ¹/₃小匙

2
中式火腿 ... ７０公克
水 １２杯
蔥 3枝
薑片 1片
酒 1大匙

1 (1600g or 3¹/₂ lbs.)duck
150g (5¹/₃oz.) ...... ground pork
100g(3¹/₂oz.) ...... wonton wrappers
6 .... bok choy (Fig. 1)
¹/₂t. .... salt

1
•1T. minced green onion
•³/₄t. sesame oil
•¹/₂t.each: soy sauce, sugar, cooking wine
•¹/₃t. salt

2
•70g(2¹/₂oz.) Chinese ham
•12C. water
•3 stalks green onion
•1 slice ginger
•1T. cooking wine

1 鴨洗淨入開水中煮開，取出洗淨；絞肉再剁細，入 **1** 料攪拌均勻再摔打至有黏性即為餡，餛飩皮包上餡，即為餛飩；火腿洗淨備用。

2 **2** 料煮開，入鴨再煮開後，改小火蓋鍋蓋燜煮 3 小時（煮時每 3 0 分鐘搖動鍋子或移動鴨身一次，以免黏鍋），取出蔥、薑及火腿，入鹽調味備用。

3 水 5 杯煮開，入餛飩煮至浮起，撈起置於鴨湯內，青江菜洗淨，整棵入開水中煮熟後亦置於鴨湯內即可。

■ 中式火腿可以火腿骨 2 0 0 公克取代；絞肉可以用五花肉來絞，油脂較多，口感較佳。

1 Wash the duck then place in boiling water, bring to a boil; remove and wash. Wonton filling: Chop the ground pork finely; mix well with **1**, throw against a counter or cutting board several times to improve the texture. Spoon filling into wonton wrappers and wrap. Wash the ham.

2 Bring **2** to a boil, add the duck and bring to a boil. Reduce to low heat, cover and simmer for 3 hours (shake the pot or turn the duck every 30 minutes to prevent sticking). Discard the green onions, ginger, and ham; season with the salt.

3 Bring 5C. water to a boil, add the wontons; cook until the wontons float. Transfer the wontons to the duck soup. Wash the bok choy and cook in boiling water until cooked; place in the duck soup. Serve.

■ Chinese ham may be substituted by 200g (7oz.) of ham bones. We recommend using pork belly for filling since it contains more fat and enhances the taste.

雞（1隻） 1100公克
蹄膀（1個） 900公克
中式火腿 600公克
鴨蛋 6個

1
水 8杯
酒 1大匙
薑片 2片
蔥 1枝

2
水 2 2杯
酒 2大匙
蔥 3枝

1100g(2½lbs., 1)chicken
900g(2lbs., 1) ....pork
shoulder
600g(1⅓lb.) ......Chinese
ham
6 ....duck eggs

1
• 8C. water
• 1T. cooking wine
• 2 slices ginger
• 1 stalk green onion

2
• 22C. water
• 2T. cooking wine
• 3 stalks green
onion

1 中式火腿洗淨蒸熟，**1**料煮開，入洗淨的蹄膀煮２５分鐘，撈起洗淨，雞洗淨，入開水中煮開後，隨即撈起再洗淨，鴨蛋煮熟後去外殼備用。

2 **2**料煮開：入蹄膀改小火煮３０分鐘，續入雞一起燉煮２小時後，入中式火腿及鴨蛋再煮３０分鐘即可。

■ 中式火腿選用蹄膀部位，且以中陳火腿較佳。

1 Wash the ham, steam until done. Bring **1** to a boil, add the washed pork shoulder and cook for 25 minutes; remove and wash again. Wash the chicken, blanch the chicken in boiling water and remove, wash again. Boil the eggs until cooked, and remove the shells.

2 Bring **2** to a boil, add the pork shoulder, reduce to low heat and cook for 30 minutes. Add the chicken and simmer for 2 hours. Mix in the ham and eggs and cook an additional 30 minutes. Serve.

■ Use the pork shoulder, part of a medium aged Chinese ham, in this recipe to increase the flavor.

兩筋一湯
Stuffed Tofu Rolls and Puffs Soup

絞肉 .... 2 2 5 公克	225g(8oz.) .... ground pork
中式火腿 .... 1 2 0 公克	120g(4¹/₃oz.) .... Chinese ham
麵筋泡（大）........ 3 0 公克	30g(1oz.) fried gluten puffs(large)
百頁 .... 1 2 張	12 sheets .... bean curd skin
高湯 .... 5 ¹/₂ 杯	5¹/₂C. .... stock

1
- 水 .... 1 ¹/₂ 大匙
- 醬油、酒 .... 各 1 ¹/₄ 小匙
- 麻油 .... ³/₄ 小匙
- 鹽 .... ¹/₃ 小匙
- 味精 .... ¹/₈ 小匙

1
- •1¹/₂t. water
- •1¹/₄t. each: soy sauce, cooking wine
- •³/₄t. sesame oil
- •¹/₃t. salt

2 糖、鹽 .... 各¹/₂ 小匙

2 •¹/₂t. each: sugar, salt

1 絞肉再剁細，入 **1** 料攪拌摔打至有黏性即為內餡，取¹/₂大匙內餡置於已處理過之百頁上，包成 5 公分長之條狀（圖 1 ）。
2 麵筋泡以熱水泡軟，再以冷水洗去大部份的油脂，瀝乾拆開，分別包入剩餘之內餡（圖 2 ），做成橄欖狀。
3 中式火腿洗淨蒸熟，切薄片，舖於小湯碗底部中間，一邊排麵筋球（圖 3 ），另一邊排百頁捲，淋上¹/₂杯高湯，蓋上保鮮膜，入鍋蒸 2 5 分鐘取出，倒出汁液扣於水盤上。
4 剩餘汁液入高湯 5 杯煮開並以 **2** 料調味，再淋於水盤中即可

1 Chop ground pork with a knife, mix well with **1** ; beat against a counter or cutting plate to improve the texture. Place ¹/₂T. filling on prepared bean curd sheets (see pg-7), wrap to make 5 cm (2") long rolls (Fig. 1).
2 Soak the fried gluten puffs in hot water until soft. Rinse with cold water to remove most of the grease, drain and split open. Fill with the remaining filling (Fig. 2) to make an oval shape.
3 Wash and steam the ham until cooked, cut into thin slices; place at the bottom center of a small soup bowl. Arrange one side with stuffed fried gluten puffs (Fig. 3); arrange the other side with bean curd sheet rolls. Pour in ¹/₂C. stock, cover the small soup bowl with cellophane paper. Steam for 25 minutes, remove; pour out the liquid and invert the soup bowl onto a large, shallow plate.
4 Bring 5C. stock and the liquid to a boil, season with **2** ; pour onto the plate, and serve.

1

2

3

片兒川
Hangzhou Style Pork Soup Noodles

陽春麵	480公克	480g(17oz.) ....plain noodles
里肌肉	280公克	280g(9¾oz.) ....pork fillet
草菇	180公克	180g(6⅓oz.) ...straw mushrooms
酸菜、韭黃	各140公克	140g(5oz.) each: ....sour mustard, yellow chives
熟筍	100公克	100g(3½oz.) ......boiled or canned bamboo shoots
中式火腿	25公克	25g(1oz.) ....Chinese ham
高湯	8杯	8C. ....stock
豬油	3大匙	3T. ....lard
鹽	½小匙	½t. ....salt

1
醬油	1小匙	•1t. soy sauce
太白粉	½小匙	•½t. cornstarch
糖	¼小匙	•¼t. sugar

2
酒、油	各2小匙	•2t. each: cooking wine, oil
鹽	1小匙	•1t. salt
糖、味精	各½小匙	•½t. sugar
胡椒粉	⅛小匙	•⅛t. pepper

1 中式火腿洗淨切片，入高湯中煮開，改小火熬煮1小時後，加水補足8杯即為上湯。
2 里肌肉切3×4公分薄片，以 **1** 料醃30分鐘後蒸熟，草菇、筍均切薄片，韭黃切段，酸菜洗淨切末均備用。
3 水10杯煮開，加鹽調味，入麵條並用筷子攪散，待麵煮開後，續入1杯冷水煮至大滾，待麵心熟透，撈出瀝乾。
4 另鍋熱入豬油3大匙燒熱，入酸菜末略炒，續入草菇、筍及上湯煮開，再以 **2** 料調味，並加麵條煮至入味後，再入韭黃及肉片即可。
■ 酸菜及韭黃可以雪裡紅取代。

1 Wash the ham and cut into slices; add the stock and bring to a boil. Reduce to low heat and cook for 1 hour. Add water when needed to keep liquid amount at 8C. This is the consommé.
2 Cut the pork fillet into 3 cm x 4 cm (1¼"x1½") slices. Marinate with **1** for 30 minutes, steam until done. Cut the mushrooms and bamboo shoots into thin slices. Cut the yellow chives into sections. Wash the sour mustard and mince; set aside to use later.
3 Bring 10C. water to a boil; season with the salt. Add the noodles, loosen with the chopsticks. After boiling, add 1C. cold water and bring to a boil, cook until the center of the noodles are thoroughly cooked. Lift out and drain.
4 Heat the wok, add 3T. lard and heat. Fry the sour mustard slightly; add the mushrooms, bamboo shoots, and consommé, then bring to a boil. Season with **2**, add noodles and heat thoroughly. Mix in the yellow chives and pork fillet and serve.
■ Sour mustard and yellow chives may be substituted with salted mustard greens.

桂花糖藕
Stuffed Lotus Roots with Osmanthus

蓮藕 6 0 0公克
圓糯米 .... $^1/_2$ 杯
桂花醬 .... $^1/_2$ 小匙

1 〔 水 .... 2 杯
     〔 冰糖 .... $^3/_4$ 杯

600g(1$^1/_3$lbs.) lotus roots
$^1/_2$C. .... short grain
glutinous rice
$^1/_2$t. .... sweet osmanthus
jam

1 〔 •2C. water
     〔 •$^3/_4$C. crystal sugar

1 圓糯米洗淨，蓮藕外皮洗淨後，從蓮藕較粗的那端切開，再由藕面之孔隙塞入圓糯米（圖1），塞糯米時須不停上下輕微震動，以利米粒充填，約7分滿後，將切開的蓋子蓋回，並用牙籤固定（圖2）。

2 蓮藕入電鍋內鍋中，加水蓋過蓮藕，入電鍋煮3小時後取出蓮藕，入另外一個鍋中再加**1**料煮開後改小火煮1小時，至濃稠再加桂花醬，取出切片排盤，再將剩餘湯汁淋於藕片上即可。

1 Wash the short grain glutinous rice and the outer layer skin of the lotus roots. Cut open the wider end of the lotus roots, which will be used as a lid piece. Stuff the holes with short grain glutinous rice (Fig. 1), shake up and down during the stuffing to slide the rice in, fill to 70% and cover with the lid piece. Close with toothpicks (Fig. 2).

2 Place the lotus roots in the inner pot of a rice cooker, cover with water, steam for 3 hours; remove the lotus roots to another pot. Add **1** and bring to a boil. Reduce to low heat and simmer for 1 hour until the sauce thickens; stir in the sweet osmanthus jam, remove. Cut the lotus roots into slices, arrange on a plate. Pour the sauce on the lotus roots and serve.

1

2

Braised Noodles with Green Onions and Dried Shrimp

陽春麵 .... 4 8 0 公克
蔥 .... 2 4 0 公克
蝦米 .... 6 0 公克
高湯 .... 8 杯
鹽 .... ¹/₂ 小匙

1 ⌈ 水 .... 3 大匙
   ⌊ 酒 .... 1 ¹/₃ 大匙

2 ⌈ 醬油 .... 2 大匙
   ⌊ 味精 .... ¹/₂ 小匙

480g(17oz.) .... plain
noodles
240g(8¹/₂oz.) .... green
onions
60g(2oz.) .....dried baby
shrimp
8C. .... stock
¹/₂t. .... salt

1 ⌈ •3T. water
   ⌊ •1¹/₃T. cooking wine

2 •2T. soy sauce

1 蝦米洗淨，入**1**料蒸 1 0 分鐘瀝乾備用，蔥洗淨切段，蔥白、蔥綠分開備用。
2 鍋熱入油 4 大匙燒熱，入蝦米炒香，續入蔥白炒至淺褐色，再入**2**料及蔥綠拌勻盛起，即為蔥油料。
3 水 1 0 杯煮開，加鹽調味，入麵條並用筷子攪散，待麵煮開後，續入 1 杯冷水煮至大滾，待麵心熟透，撈出瀝乾。
4 砂鍋內入高湯煮開，再入麵條煮 **3** 分鐘，續入蔥油料燜煮 5 分鐘即可。

1 Wash the dried baby shrimp, add **1**, steam for 10 minutes, and drain. Wash the green onions, cut into sections; separate the green and white sections.
2 Heat the wok, add 4T. oil and heat. Fry the dried baby shrimp until fragrant. Add the white sections of the green onions and fry until light brown. Season with **2** and add the green sections of the green onions. Mix well and set aside.
3 Bring 10C. water to a boil, season with the salt. Stir in the noodles, use chopsticks to loosen the noodles, and cook until boiling. Add another 1C. cold water, bring to a boil again. Remove noodles from pot when transparent.
4 Bring the stock to a boil in a Ceramic pot. Stir in the noodles and cook for 3 minutes. Add the green onion sauce, cover and simmer for 5 minutes. Serve.

酒釀湯圓
Sweet Wine Rice with Dough Balls

香蕉、橘子瓣各１００公克	100g(3½ oz.) each: .... bananas, oranges
糖、酒釀 各４大匙	4T. each: ..sugar, fermented wine rice
芝麻湯圓 １２個	12 .... sesame seeds rice dough balls
蛋 ２個	2 .... eggs

1 香蕉切成０.３立方公分小丁,橘子瓣切半備用。
2 水４杯煮開,入湯圓煮至浮起,撈出置湯碗中。
3 另水４杯煮開,入糖、香蕉、橘子煮開熄火,續入打散之蛋液及酒釀拌勻,再沖入置湯圓的湯碗中即可。
■ 可用罐頭橘子取代新鮮橘子。

1 Cut the bananas into 0.3 cm (⅛") cubes, cut the orange wedges into halves.
2 Bring 4C. water to a boil. Cook the sesame seeds rice dough balls until they float; remove and place in a soup bowl.
3 Bring another 4C. water to a boil; add the sugar, bananas, and oranges. Turn off heat after boiling. Mix the beaten eggs and fermented wine rice thoroughly, pour into the soup bowl with the sesame seeds rice dough balls.
■ Canned mandarin oranges may be substituted with fresh oranges.

菜飯
Vegetable Rice

青江菜 ９００公克	900g(2lbs.) .... bok choy
蓬萊米 ３杯	3C. .... short grain rice
雞油 ６大匙	6T. .... chicken fat
醬油 ２小匙	2t. .... soy sauce
1 ┌ 鹽 ....１½小匙 └ 味精 １小匙	**1** •1½ t. salt

1 青江菜洗淨切長段。鍋熱入雞油燒熱,入青江菜炒軟(不必全熟),並加**1**料調味後,青江菜盛出,菜湯留用。
2 米洗淨瀝乾,加醬油拌勻,再加菜湯及水共３杯,入青江菜一起拌勻後,置電鍋內鍋中,外鍋加水２杯,煮至開關跳起後,續燜１０分鐘即可。
■ 若無雞油,可以用沙拉油６大匙取代。

1 Wash and cut the bok choy into long sections. Heat the wok, add the chicken fat and heat. Fry the bok choy until soft (does not need to be well done), season with **1** ; remove the bok choy. Keep the vegetable soup for later use.
2 Wash the rice, drain, stir in the soy sauce thoroughly; add a total of 3C. vegetable soup and water. Mix in the bok choy. Place the mixture in the inner pot of a rice cooker, add 2C. water into the outer part of the rice cooker. Cook until switch jumps up, wait for 10 additional minutes, and serve.
■ Chicken fat may be substituted with 6T. vegetable oil.

Pork and Vegetable Wonton Soup

小白菜 250公克
餛飩皮 150公克
絞肉 100公克
蛋 .... 1/2 個
雞高湯 .... 6 杯

1
麻油 .... 2 小匙
醬油 .... 1 小匙
鹽 .... 1/4 小匙
味精 .... 1/8 小匙

2
榨菜末 ...... 4 大匙
蝦米末 ...... 1 大匙
醬油 .... 1 小匙
鹽 .... 3/4 小匙
麻油 .... 1/2 小匙
味精 .... 1/4 小匙

250g(9oz.) .... baby
cabbage
150g(5¹/₄oz.) ...... wonton
wrappers
100g(3¹/₂oz.) .... ground
pork
¹/₂ .... egg
6C. .... chicken broth

1
•2t. sesame oil
•1t. soy sauce
•¹/₄t. salt

2
•4T. minced pickled
mustard head
•1T. minced dried
shrimp
•1t. soy sauce
•³/₄t. salt
•¹/₂t. sesame oil

1 絞肉再剁細,加 **1** 料拌勻,小白菜洗淨,入開水中煮熟後取出剁碎並擠乾水份,與絞肉攪拌摔打,使之具有黏性,即為內餡。
2 將每張餛飩皮包入 1 份內餡,先對折成三角形,再折成半,最後兩角對疊成形,即為餛飩。
3 鍋熱塗上一層油,入打散之蛋液煎成蛋皮,待涼,切細絲。
4 雞高湯煮開,入餛飩煮至浮起,再入 **2** 料拌勻,熄火,起鍋,灑上蛋皮絲即可。
■ 小白菜可以青江菜取代;絞肉可以用五花肉來絞,油脂較多,口感較佳。

1 Wonton filling: Chop ground pork finely, mix in **1**. Wash baby cabbages, cook in boiling water until done; remove and chop finely, and squeeze dry. Mix well with ground pork and throw against a counter or cutting board several times to improve the texture.
2 Wrap each wonton wrapper with 1 serving of filling, then fold into triangular shape. Fold in half and pinch together the two corners.
3 Heat the wok, brush the surface with oil. Fry the beaten eggs to make egg crepes; cool and cut into thin strips.
4 Bring the chicken broth to a boil, add the wontons and boil until they float. Mix in **2** and turn off the heat. Sprinkle top with egg strips and serve.
■ Baby cabbages may be substituted with bok choy. Ground pork belly is preferred over ground lean pork; pork belly is fattier and tastier.

Publishing

Taiwan, R.O.C. Tel : (02)507-4902

麵食·精華篇
- 87道菜
- 96頁
- 中英對照
- 平裝250元

Noodles
Classical Cooking
- 87 recipes
- 96 pages
- Chinese/English Bilingual

麵食·家常篇
- 91道菜
- 96頁
- 中英對照
- 平裝250元

Noodles
Home Cooking
- 91 recipes
- 96 pages
- Chinese/English Bilingual

米食·傳統篇
- 82道菜
- 96頁
- 中英對照
- 平裝250元

Rice
Traditional Cooking
- 82 recipes
- 96 pages
- Chinese/English Bilingual

米食·家常篇
- 84道菜
- 96頁
- 中英對照
- 平裝250元

Rice
Home Cooking
- 84 recipes
- 96 pages
- Chinese/English Bilingual

嬰幼兒食譜
- 140道菜
- 104頁
- 中文版
- 平裝250元

Baby & Children Cooking
- 140 recipes
- 104 pages
- Chinese

飲茶食譜
- 88道菜
- 128頁
- 中英對照
- 平裝300元
  精裝350元

Chinese Dim Sum
- 88 recipes
- 128 pages
- Chinese/English Bilingual

素食
- 84道菜
- 116頁
- 中英對照
- 平裝250元
  精裝300元

Vegetarian Cooking
- 84 recipes
- 116 pages
- Chinese/English Bilingual

家常100
- 100道菜
- 96頁
- 中英對照
- 平裝250元

Favorite Chinese Dishes
- 100 recipes
- 96 pages
- Chinese/English Bilingual

味全家政班

味全家政班創立於民國五十年，經過三十餘年的努力，它不只是國內歷史最悠久的家政研習班，更成為一所正式學制之外的家政專門學校。

創立之初，味全家政班以教授中國菜及研習烹飪技術為主，因教學成果良好，備受各界讚譽，乃於民國五十二年，增闢插花、工藝、美容等各門專科，精湛的師資，教學內容的充實，深獲海內外的肯定與好評。

三十餘年來，先後來班參與研習的學員已近二十萬人次，學員的足跡遍及台灣以外，更有許多國外的團體或個人專程抵台，到味全家政班求教，在習得中國菜烹調的精髓後，或返回居住地經營餐飲業，或擔任家政教師，或獲聘為中國餐廳主廚者大有人在，成就倍受激賞。

近年來，味全家政班亟力研究開發改良中國菜餚，並深入國際間，採集各種精緻、道地美食，除了樹立中華文化「食的精神」外，並將各國烹飪口味去蕪存菁，擷取地方特色。為了確保這些研究工作更加落實，我們特將這些集合海內外餐飲界與研發單位的精典之作，以縝密的拍攝技巧與專業編輯，出版各式食譜，以做傳承。

薪傳與發揚中國烹飪的藝術，是味全家政班一貫的理念，日後，也將秉持宗旨，永續不輟。

Wei-Chuan
Cooking School

Since its establishment in 1961, Wei-Chuan Cooking School has made a continuous commitment to improving and modernizing the culinary art of cooking and special skills training. As a result, it is the oldest and most successful school of its kind in Taiwan.

In the beginning, Wei-Chuan Cooking School was primarily teaching and researching Chinese cooking techniques. However, due to popular demand, the curriculum was expanded to cover courses in flower arrangements, handcrafts, beauty care, dress making and many other specialized fields by 1963.

The fact that almost 200,000 students, from Taiwan and other countries all over the world, have matriculated in this school can be directly attributed to the high quality of the teaching staff and the excellent curriculum offered to the students. Many of the graduates have become successful restaurant owners and chefs, and in numerous cases, respected teachers.

While Wei-Chuan Cooking School has always been committed to developing and improving Chinese cuisine, we have recently extended our efforts toward gathering information and researching recipes from different provinces of China. With the same dedication to accuracy and perfection as always, we have begun to publish these authentic regional gourmet recipes for our devoted readers. These new publications will continue to reflect the fine tradition of quality our public has grown to appreciate and expect.